CW01670083

Vegetables for Vision

Nature's Supplements for Eye Health

Ian Grierson PhD FRCPath

Professor of Ophthalmology,
University of Liverpool

Hon Professor of Optometry,
University of Wales, Cardiff

To my mother, Gwen, who was a school dinner lady who could cook! More than a few of the recipes in this book are down to her and to my wife, Dee, who was so good about all the mess I made in our kitchen while checking out some of the recipes. Also a number of the recipes I've included were 'stolen' from Dee and her family.

Acknowledgements

With grateful thanks to: The Macular Disease Society whose support has been crucial for the completion of this book. I was encouraged to start this enterprise by my friends at the Wirral Society of the Blind and Partially Sighted. The Foundation for Prevention of Blindness in Liverpool has been my support for well over 10 years whether it be eye science or vegetable recipes. I would like to single out for particular thanks Tom Bremridge and Gwyn Dickinson (MDS); Sue Hadley; Joan Davies and Lynne Sedgewick (WBPS); Simon Harding and Tom Sutherland (FFPB). Many thanks also to the 'mixed case' and Brian Weaton my long suffering wine tutor.

Design: indigo creative marketing

Illustrations: L E Davies

Published by: 1st edition 2005, indigo creative marketing
2nd edition 2008, indigo creative marketing
PO Box 246, Crowborough, East Sussex TN6 9BU

ISBN: 978-0-9551131-0-9

Contents

Background Information

Introduction

Advances in medicine coupled with better hygiene have made a huge difference to life expectancy but mostly in the Western World. About 100 years ago less than 1% of the people in the World were over 65 years of age. By the middle of the present century the number of over 65-year-olds is estimated to be about 20% of the population. If 1 in 5 of us rather than 1 in 100 of us are reaching the current retirement age, surely that can only be considered to be a great bonus? On the other hand a longer life span is only a wonderful thing if it is accompanied by good health. The problem of course is that quality of life is compromised by a large number of age-related illnesses. These include a host of ailments of all types such as arthritis, diabetes, chest problems, incontinence, brittle bones, stroke, senility and, not surprisingly, depression.

Hearing and sight loss can also be age-associated. In a survey of the sighted elderly, high on the list, if not top, of the age-related problems they wished to avoid most of all was blindness. In the human population, blindness has an extremely high fear ratio. It is suggested by sociologists and psychiatrists that we fear blindness more than death. There is even a phobia of blindness that is called scotomaphobia. The reality of course is somewhat different from the phobia. Blind and partially sighted people are, on the whole incredibly adaptable, resilient and capable. People who are completely blind fortunately are rare but those with a significant visual disability are much more common and particularly common among the elderly. A highly significant ailment that robs the elderly in our society of their sight is Age-Related Macular Degeneration or AMD.

Features of AMD

Macular degeneration can be separated into early and late onset disease that attacks a specific part of the retina of the eye called the macula. The Macular Disease Society and the Royal National Institute for the Blind (RNIB) have excellent pamphlets explaining AMD and I can highly recommend them to those of you who have AMD, have loved ones with AMD or are simply interested in AMD.

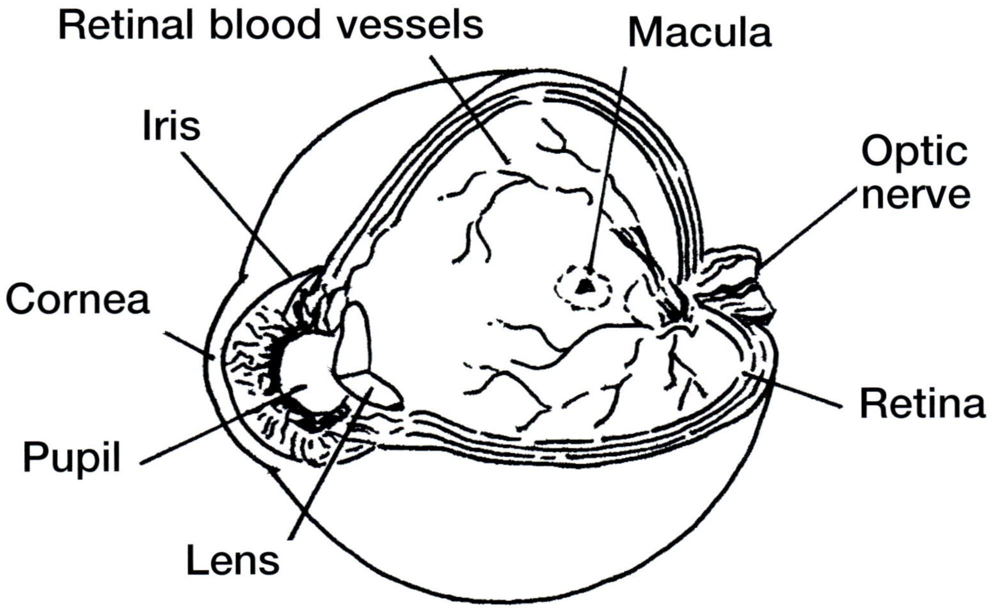

Figure 1

The macula is a small spot in the retina (Figure 1). It is delicate and vulnerable and most concerned with central vision. The cone type of photoreceptor dominates the macula and they are concerned with high quality daylight sight. If the support tissues for the macular photoreceptors fail, the macula perishes and, with its loss of function, there is loss of central vision.

The late onset form of macular degeneration is better known as Age-Related Macular Degeneration or AMD, and AMD is the most common cause of blindness in the UK accounting for around 50% of all blind registrations. It also is the most common cause of blind registration in all the countries of the Western World. As is the case with all the age-associated eye diseases, the numbers of people with AMD are increasing and predicted to get much higher in the near future. What is not so clear is whether the increase in AMD is simply the result of there being more elderly people or whether there is a further underlying trend for an increase in this disease beyond a straight forward age shift in our population. There is still so much we don't know about AMD but all the signs are that we are faced in the immediate future with a situation that may be worse in terms of numbers of sufferers than the present with less than ideal treatments.

AMD sufferers are usually divided up into having one of two forms of the disease – dry or wet.

The dry form develops slowly and involves a general deterioration of the support tissue that maintains the macula. In many ways the dry form can be considered as an exaggeration of normal ageing events that go on in the retinal tissues. It is estimated that as many as 90% of AMD patients have this type of degeneration.

The wet form has a far more rapid onset and is associated with the development of a vascularised scar-like sheet under or around the macula. Eye doctors call the vascular sheet a choroidal neovascular (CNV) membrane and divide them into classic and occult forms based on the way the membranes develop. Where exactly the CNV membrane develops in relation to the macula and how quickly it develops can have a profound influence on treatment options if there are any!

Prevention

We cannot cure AMD and will not be able to do so in the immediate future. Then what about doing something early enough to prevent or at least delay the onset of the degeneration? Prevention is all about identifying risk factors for a disease and addressing them where possible. Risk factors can be subdivided into those over which we have some control and those we can't do anything about.

Table 1 is a list of some of the more obvious factors to consider.

Table 1 – Risk Factors for AMD

1. **Age –** it is self evident that a major risk factor if not the major risk factor for AMD is age. People in their fifties have a 1 in 50 chance of getting AMD whereas if you are over 75 then 1 in 4 or even 1 in 3 will get the disease.
2. **Family history –** there is a greater risk of developing AMD if a close relative is or was a sufferer. The genetics of AMD are not simple, however, and many patients have no obvious family history.
3. **Personal history –** AMD in one eye increases the risk of having the disease in the 2nd eye.
4. **Gender –** there are more women with AMD than men.
5. **Race –** Caucasians seem to be more prone than other races.
6. **Hyperopia –** long sightedness is associated with AMD to the extent that a long-sighted person has a 50% greater risk of developing AMD than someone with normal sight.
7. **Sunlight –** excessive exposure to strong sunlight is thought to be a risk factor for AMD but the relationship is not entirely clear.
8. **Blood pressure –** there is evidence that hypertension and high cholesterol increase the risk of AMD. A history of heart disease or stroke is also a risk factor.
9. **Body weight –** heavy people are at greater risk of developing AMD than people below or at their recommended body weight.
10. **Smoking –** is an important risk factor that has been shown clearly to promote earlier onset of AMD. It has been shown that smoking more than 20 cigarettes a day increases the risk of AMD between two and three fold. Unfortunately a large French study suggests that the risk of AMD remains high even after a person has given up the habit.
11. **Alcohol –** it is not at all clear how important alcohol is as a risk factor for AMD; however, we know that excessive drinking is a general health risk.
12. **Diet –** a diet poor in key antioxidant vitamins, vegetables and fruit creates a greater risk of AMD and accelerates the progress of the disease.

I have listed the main risk factors and of these we are not able to do much about the first 5 on the list, but the remainder can be addressed.

It is absolutely clear that smoking is bad news for a lot of things and AMD is on that ever growing list. It is good sense that people with AMD wear sunglasses when they are in strong sunlight to avoid further deterioration in their central vision from harmful rays.

Excessive alcohol intake gets and deserves a bad press. However, there are no clear cut results to show a relationship between alcohol consumption and incidence of AMD; but because heavy and routine alcohol intake is bad for health in general then moderation is advisable. It may be seen as perverse that I have suggested an appropriate wine with many of the recipes in this book. My motivation is to make the dishes as pleasant as possible especially if they are being prepared for special occasions. I am not at all suggesting that wine is healthy, but it is nice, and the trick is to prefer quality not quantity.

If you are very heavy then try to do something about it but I worry about getting too obsessive and some diets can do as much harm as good. Personally I think the main thing is to eat the right type of food and, unless your weight is endangering your general health, then don't get fixated with 'body mass indexes'– just use your common sense. Obsession with body mass index is a current fad in the USA where it is referred to as BMI. At first I mistakenly thought this to be a reference to a British Airline. Blood pressure on the other hand is life threatening as well as sight threatening and needs to be under control. Something none of us can afford to be slipshod about. The last risk factor in the list is poor diet and that is the subject of the rest of this book.

Diet Matters

In this book I have tried to provide some background and further information on AMD but by doing this I am merely trying to put my main objective into context. The point I really want to make is that healthy eating can make a difference. Eating more of what is good for you and less of what is not so good is no radical approach.

I am too much of a junk-food junky on the sly (first in line for fish and chips or hot dogs) to be so hypocritical as to suggest anything drastic for others. Healthy eating may seem too much of a lifestyle change especially if you equate healthy eating with boring eating. Many of us hate vegetables in general and green leafy vegetables in particular from bad eating experiences in childhood. For my part I can still hear my granny saying, 'Eat up your greens before you leave the table.'

If you have a vegetable phobia and you are thinking, 'You can keep your rabbit food if that is what you are proposing' – well, I am not proposing you eat veg despite the taste. What I am suggesting is that you can take many vegetables that have a bad press and do something with them that is really quite nice.

Great platefuls of soggy boiled greens, cabbage and spinach may be some people's idea of foody heaven but it is not mine. I am not a nutrition expert by any means. I am merely a slightly overweight scientist with an interest in AMD who enjoys cooking for relaxation.

Having said all this, I cannot ignore the fact that it is the very vegetables that many of us loathe that top the healthy list. The ones with difficult textures and flavours are the very ones that have all the goodies in them that are considered to be so beneficial for health and good for eyes, and have properties that combat the development and progress of AMD.

Clearly green leafy vegetables (or GLVs) are rich in goodness but they have not got a monopoly on healthy nutrients – there are alternatives. Also it may well be that you don't like GLVs simply because you have not had them in the right context or recipe for you. For that matter the common vegetables that you have every day may well provide the necessary antioxidants and macular protectants, but you simply don't eat enough of them to make a difference either to general health or eye health. The main section of this book lists recipes you may like to try but they are only a limited set of examples that might help you form the beginnings of an interesting diet where vegetables (and fruit) play a more prominent part than before.

The recipes are not included because they are nutritionally well balanced (way beyond me I'm afraid to say). This is not a slimmer's bible either because there are lots of calories in some of my offerings. They do not follow a particular style or cooking fad. The recipes are just ones I have collected or adapted over the years that my family likes (on the whole). They are intended as a stimulus to eat more veg, particularly GLVs and the other AMD foods. If you eat lots of vegetables already then just try some of these recipes for fun and see how they stack up against your own favourites.

I have emphasised vegetables but it is important to point out that fruit, meat, fish, cereals, nuts etc. all have nutrient components that are reputed to give visual benefit. Balance is the key as with many things.

The goodies from the diet that are important for the macula are antioxidant vitamins, carotenes and key minerals. The most relevant vitamins to the macula are vitamins C, A and E (Table 2). Table 2 also lists some of the foods rich in these antioxidant vitamins.

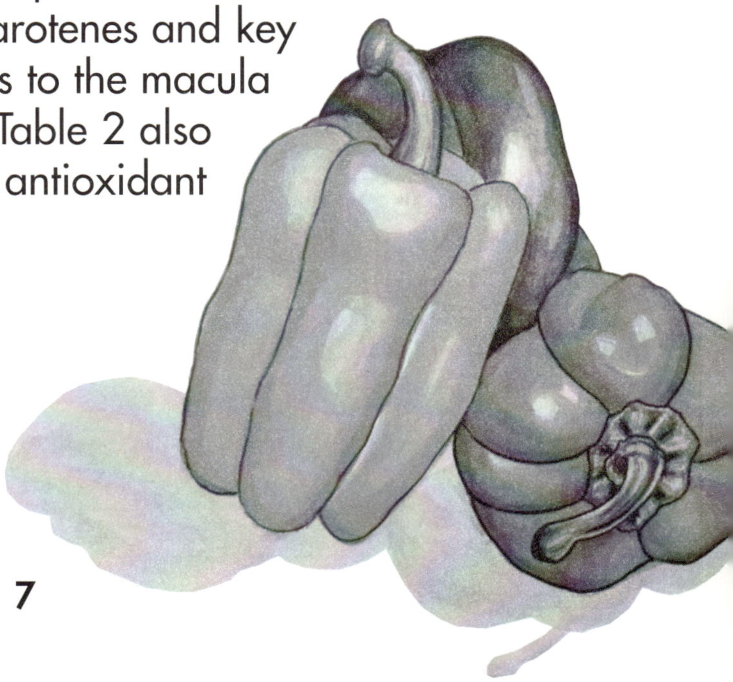

Table 2 – The Antioxidant Vitamins

Vitamin C (40mg per day intake)

It helps the body produce collagen and to absorb iron as well as having an antioxidant protective role so important to macular survival. It is a water-soluble vitamin and therefore easily lost during vigorous cooking. Present in a wide variety of vegetables and fruit including spinach, broccoli, tomatoes, oranges, lemons.

Vitamin E (4mg for men and 3mg for women per day – a reasonable and safe intake)

It keeps skin healthy and is the key antioxidant that copes with the free radicals generated at and around the macula. It is a fat-soluble vitamin present in vegetables, vegetable oils, nuts, cereals, fish and chicken.

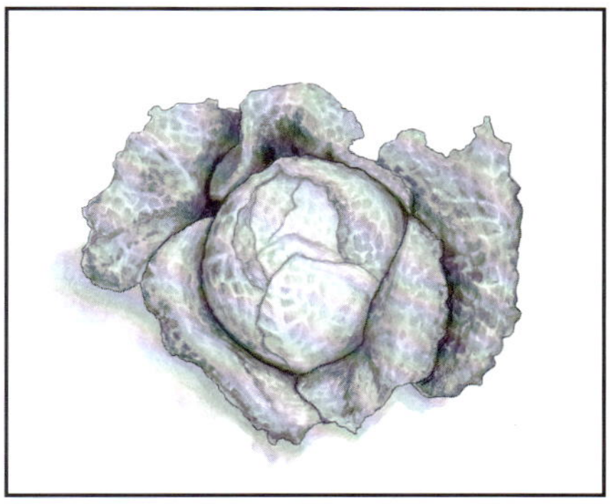

Vitamin A (700µg for men and 600µg for women per day)

Often referred to as the 'eye vitamin' but it also keeps the body linings in good condition. A fat-soluble vitamin that is stable. Found in carrots, green leafy veg (GLVs), tomatoes, oranges, apricots, mango (orange-coloured fruit).

Carotenoids

We seem to need a wide range of carotenoids in our diet to maintain health (Table 3) and these are provided by an equally impressive range of foods. The macula is rich in two carotenoids called lutein and zeaxanthin. These macular pigments are pivotal to the macula's defences against free radical attack and toxic damage. In addition the macular carotenes have a yellowish colour and filter out potentially harmful blue light from the total light that is focused at the macula by the lens. Lutein and zeaxanthin are thought to be depleted in sufferers with AMD. Whether the low levels of macular pigments are a consequence of the degeneration in AMD or are actually a causal or contributory factor to the disease process is not entirely clear. It has to be said that the balance of scientific opinion is leaning towards there being a causal link.

Table 3 Common Carotenes

Alpha carotene – gives rise to Vitamin A in the body. An even more effective anticancer agent than the beta form. An antioxidant.
Present in carrots, coriander, tomatoes, green beans, GLVs.

Beta carotene – also gives rise to Vitamin A. Acts as an anti-cancer agent. In carrots, spinach, GLVs, peaches, apricots.

Lutein – the main macular pigment. Present in GLVs.
See Table 4.

Lycopene – associated with tomatoes and tomato products.

Cryptoxanthin – a rich source is found in oranges.

Zeaxanthin – The second macular pigment. Not particularly prominent in GLVs but abundant in colourful vegetables like sweetcorn, peppers etc.

We need significant amounts of each of the carotenes but can have our body store drastically deleted by bad health and poor diet. Synthetic forms are not as effective as natural forms nor are they absorbed as well. There are more than 600 natural carotenoids.

The yellow carotenes of the macula, lutein and zeaxanthin, seem to have many protective functions. As a result it seems to be a sensible approach to boost macular carotene levels in patients or even those at risk of developing AMD. It has been shown that elderly people who have retained good central vision usually have particularly high lutein and zeaxanthin levels in their maculas. Our bodies do not make lutein so all that we have in and around the macula come from the diet. Adults in the UK have a very variable intake of lutein that is estimated for most to be only 1mg per day. The amount of lutein that the experts say will make a health difference is around 4mg per day but up to around 6 to 10mg (or even more) is better. There is a huge shortfall that has to be down to us and the way we live.

To make a big difference to your lutein levels you do not have to be shovelling in platefuls of rabbit food: ½ a cup (around 75ml or 5 tbsps) of cooked spinach will give you 6mg of lutein per day, well into the healthy range. The vegetables rich in lutein are listed in Table 4. It is now known that either eating vegetables rich in lutein or taking lutein supplement preparations will increase blood levels of this substance, but more importantly macular pigmentation seems to be boosted. Dietary modification towards higher intake of antioxidant vitamins and lutein appears to be a sensible approach to combat AMD, but should it be by food or supplement intake?

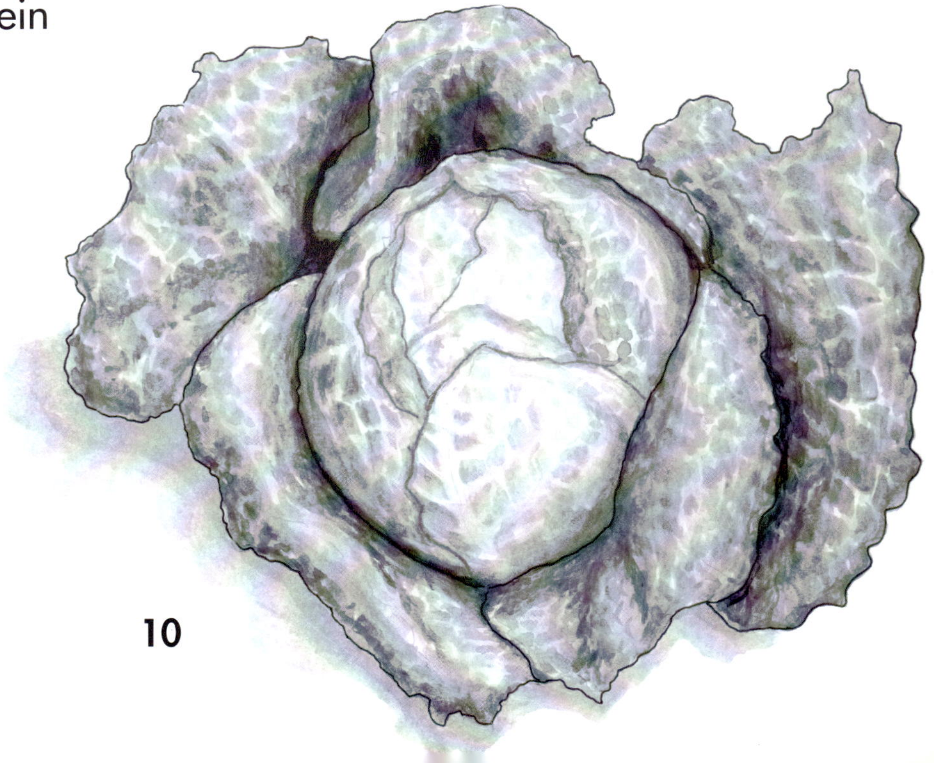

Table 4 – Selected Vegetables Rich in Lutein

Vegetable	Lutein Content (mcg/100g)
Kale	22,000
Curly cabbage	16,500
Spinach	12,500
Cress	12,500
Winter greens	11,000
Chicory	10,000
Okra	7,000
Pepper (red)	7,000
Endive	4,000
Celery	3,500
Leaf lettuce	2,000
Leek	2,000
Broccoli	2,000
Peas	1,700

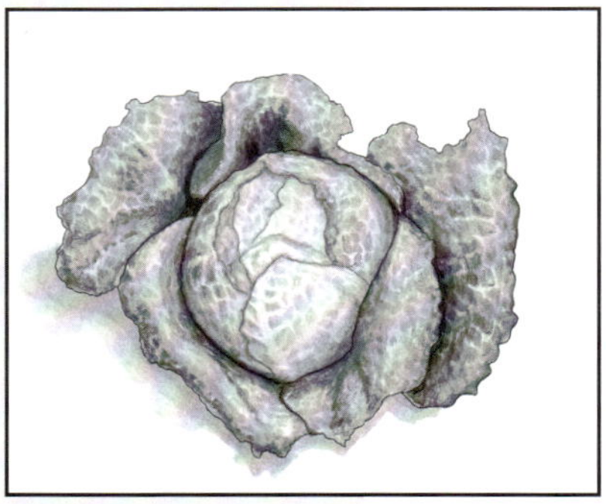

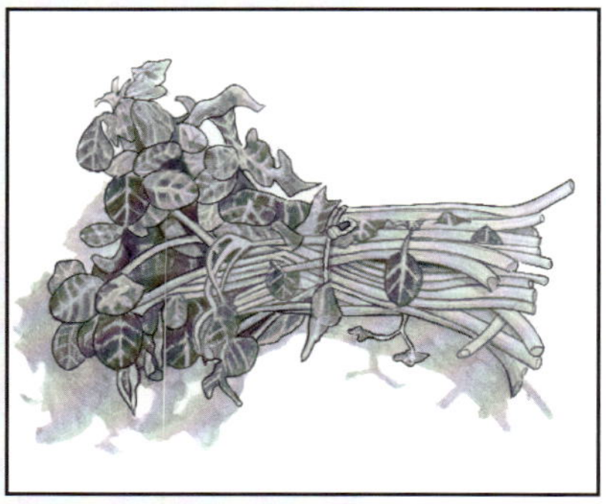

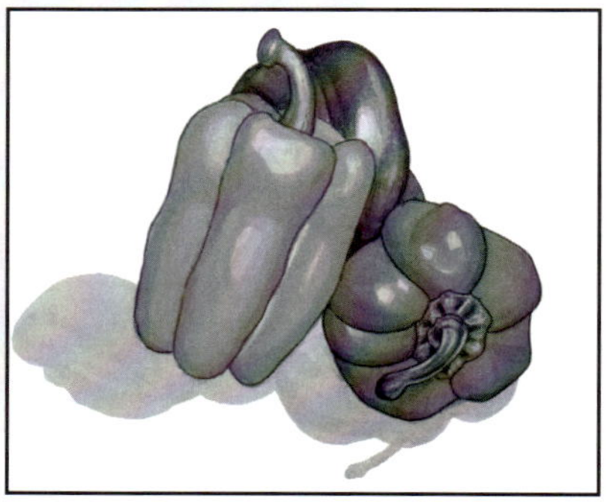

Supplements

A reasonable question to ask is, 'Why bother with nasty vegetables when there are perfectly good supplements containing the appropriate vitamins and carotenoids to be had from supermarkets, health shops and even the internet.' All of this is true of course. At one time the evidence for the effectiveness of supplements in combating AMD was at best confusing and at worst the published findings were often contradictory. More recent and more appropriately designed investigations show that at least some supplement mixtures retard the development of AMD.

Currently there are large numbers of supplement preparations available on the market that claim to be of medical and visual benefit to both those who have AMD and those who may be at risk of developing AMD (Table 5). The preparations are marketed on the one hand by the large pharmaceutical companies like Bausch & Lomb, Alcon and Novartis. However, there are also small scale suppliers selling everything from artificial antioxidant combinations through to alternative medicine preparations often via the internet. The major impetus for eye specialists, nutritionalists and AMD sufferers to have a reawakened enthusiasm for supplements are the statistically significant findings of a number of clinical studies, the most influential being the AREDS trial.

Table 5 – A shortened list of some of the many eye health supplements marketed as being of benefit to AMD patients

VisiVite	Ocuvite (AREDS formula)
Ocudyne	Ocuvite Extra
Bright Eyes	ICaps
Ocuguard plus	Macusan
EyeVites	Viteyes
Maxivision	Vitalux Plus
OptimEyes	

AREDS stands for Age-Related Eye Disease Study and this 5 year investigation involved 5,000 people aged between 55 and 80 years of age. They were selected on the basis of having no AMD, early AMD, middle-stage AMD and advanced disease. For people at high risk of developing advanced AMD that risk was reduced by 25% with a mixture of antioxidant vitamins and zinc. The ingredients of the supplement mixture are listed in Table 6. If, however, the subjects had no AMD or very mild AMD then no clear benefit was shown.

Table 6 – The AREDS Supplement Mixture daily dose (Bausch & Lomb)

Vitamin C – 500mg	Zinc (oxide) – 80mg
Vitamin E – 400 IU	Copper (cupric oxide) – 2mg
Beta Carotene – 15mg	

The clear message from this study is that the AREDS mixture has a significant benefit for those AMD patients at risk of developing severe end stage AMD regardless of whether the patient has the wet or dry form. Those patients considering going on to supplements should do so only after consultation with their GP or specialist. It should be noted that the antioxidant concentrations in the AREDS supplement ranges from 5 to 15 times the recommended daily intake of these substances. A further important point that should be taken on board is that neither lutein nor zeaxanthin was included in the AREDS supplement. In the light of what we now know about the key role of lutein and zeaxanthin in macular protection the AREDS mixture is far from being the perfect AMD supplement. As a result many of the marketed supplement mixtures include lutein as well as the antioxidant vitamins.

The high levels of antioxidants in supplements come with a down side. There is evidence that smokers who take beta carotene have an elevated risk of lung cancer. Indeed it is recommended that smokers do not use the marketed versions of the AREDS formula but use a smoker's version where the beta carotene has been replaced by lutein or other additives. High levels of vitamin E such as those present in many of the mega-dose supplements can aggravate bleeding disorders. In general high doses of any vitamin can alter the absorption of other vitamins or interfere with the effectiveness of some medications that the elderly patient might be taking to treat an unrelated condition. Zinc is useful to the eye but it depletes body copper, hence the need in the AREDS formula to provide additional copper in the supplement mixture.

Continuing concerns about high doses in the AREDS formula and an absence of the key antioxidants, lutein and zeaxanthin have lead to the initiation of an AREDS2 trial, which is ongoing and will not report until 2011 at least. AREDS2 will look at the effects of supplements containing lutein, zeaxanthin and also omega-3 on AMD and cataract development. It will also re-examine the AREDS formula by reducing zinc and eliminating beta carotene.

It would be wrong to paint too lurid a picture but there is concern among eye specialists that the unmonitored use of high dose supplements for a long time is not wise. Most people, however, think that the health risk of antioxidant supplements is minimal. 'Foodies' make the point that the supplements are expensive, many of them contain components that have not been carefully evaluated as yet and, if the antioxidants are artificial preparations, the body does not absorb them at all well. 'Pill poppers' state that foods that are good for you are usually not nice to eat or at the very best they are boring. Fat soluble vitamins like A and E are most abundant in oils and fats – if you have too much, they are not very healthy for you and, if very large amounts of antioxidant are needed, then supplements are really the only way to do that.

It comes back to the food versus pills argument we started with. There is still no professional acceptance of the universal value of AMD supplements, whereas I know most eye specialists when advising newly diagnosed patients with AMD, suggest that, if the patients are not already on a diet rich in fresh vegetables and fruit, they should try it out. Vegetables, fruit, cereals and appropriate meats provide you with a steady intake of antioxidant vitamins and carotenoids at 'natural' but not at the huge supplement levels. It may well be that high supplement levels of antioxidants make a difference to AMD progression but constant intake is not appropriate for everyone.

A 'good' balanced vegetable and fruit-rich diet should be for everyone but vegetables have a 'bad press'. I have tried, through a number of home recipes, to make the important eye health vegetables a lot more palatable and a little less boring. We are not dealing with rocket science here. Believe me if I can cook it, you can cook it! In our family my wife Dee is the only one to have been to cookery classes and she is the star. I enjoy cooking, I have travelled a lot and I like different cuisines, but only just get by in the kitchen. I've kept to what are relatively simple and quick recipes (because that is all I can manage), so give at least some of them a try!

Wine

I have a small wine cellar in my house and have developed an interest in wines as a hobby. Subsequently I could not resist trying to fit an appropriate wine with the main meals. Alcohol in excess is bad news for health in general and is a possible risk factor of a number of eye conditions, so I am not advocating that you become wine or other alcohol enthusiasts. A case has been made in the press and elsewhere that a little wine can be a good thing but such an argument can be taken too far.

It is true that wines, especially red wines, have a high phenol and flavonoid content. Moderate drinkers in a few key studies seem to have a lower risk of dying from some cancers. It is also the case that polyphenols can reduce heart disease by combating dietary fats and cholesterol. It is thought by many health experts, but not proven, that the French enthusiasms for red wine explains why they seem to be able to eat fatty food but are less prone to heart problems than the British. My own belief is that the red wine explanation for the 'French phenomenon' is too good to be true and undoubtedly too simplistic. Evidence might suggest there is an advantage in choosing a red wine rather than a beer with dinner if you are so inclined. However, if you don't drink alcohol, then the health attraction of modest wine drinking with meals is too minor to be of consequence and there are very reasonable alternatives.

I like to think that a little wine can make a good meal special. As a major objective of the book is to make vegetable dishes as attractive as possible, then my wine tips are just a trivial embellishment. The wine selection is an addition that can be taken on board at an appropriate occasion or simply ignored. The selection can be ignored because I am not an expert and a professional would without doubt come up with a better match than mine. It is not appropriate always to have wine with meals but, when you want to, drink the wine you like not what some wine snob tells you. Even if you are 'sold' on the health advantage of red wines, I have to say that in my opinion white wines are often the best mates for vegetable-rich meals but they have less phenols. Wines are for enjoyment not health and alcohol-free wines, red grape juices or even a handful of raisins carry all the same benefits as phenol-rich red wines.

Asparagus

Asparagus

According to the botany books asparagus is some sort of lily or at least it belongs to the lily family of plants. In England it is usual to grow green asparagus whereas on the Continent white seems to predominate in some regions. White asparagus is merely standard asparagus grown under cover. Asparagus is rich in minerals and has some antioxidant vitamins in addition. Remember that the spears are delicate at their tips and coarse further away, so it is best to trim away the stalks unless you really are an asparagus fan. Traditionally asparagus is cooked in a deep pan as a bunch with the stalks in the water and the tips well out but covered with tin foil. Heat the pan and the stalks will be boiled and the tips will steam; this will take around 20 minutes or more. Hard boil with the lid on the pan.

Asparagus rolls

Cooked asparagus doesn't need much to make it special to my mind. Just a little brown bread and butter is all that is necessary, but the bread has to be a favourite type and very fresh. Asparagus rolls work fine with asparagus out of a jar but the fresh variety has more goodness in it.

Makes around 50 mini rolls.

300–400g (10–13oz) can or jar of white
or green asparagus tips, or
450g (1lb) of fresh asparagus tips as an alternative
in season in spring/summer
100g (4oz) smoked salmon slices (optional)
1 large sliced wholemeal loaf
Butter or favourite spread

1. Cook fresh asparagus as previously stated in boiling water for 8 minutes.
2. Drain the asparagus and allow to cool
   (or take straight from the jar or can).
3. Take bread and with a rolling pin spread out until thin.
4. Butter (or use an alternative) and cut off crusts if you wish.
5. Line up asparagus end to end on one long edge of the bread.

6. Place the roll with the join underneath on large plate.
7. Repeat until the plate is full and place in fridge until required (same day is best).
8. Cut each roll into about three pieces.
9. Garnish each roll with a sliver of smoked salmon (optional) and serve.

You will have made enough for guests but please do cut the quantities if required, particularly if you are using fresh asparagus as it can get so expensive out of season. A white wine is best but my favourite with asparagus rolls or simply asparagus on its own is Vouvray. Vouvray comes from the Loire in France and it is made from the chenin blanc grape. The Loire valley is wall-to-wall with asparagus in the spring so Vouvray is in my opinion a well-suited partner.

Asparagus and potato salad

This recipe requires fresh asparagus. When you buy long spears, there can be considerable waste chopping off the ends, but these can be used. If the ends are boiled up with scrubbed new potatoes they can form the basis of a nutritious and healthy salad which is lovely and tasty.

Makes 4 portions

450g (1lb) of fresh green asparagus spears
1½ kg (3¼ lb) scrubbed new potatoes (don't peel them because the vitamin content is highest in the skin)
Mixed salad leaves
Low calorie mayonnaise or vinaigrette

1. Cut off the tips of the asparagus and cook separately for 8 minutes.
2. Cut stalks in half and mix with the new potatoes.
3. Boil the potatoes and asparagus stalks in salted water for at least 30 minutes or until the stalks and potatoes are soft.
4. Drain, cool and chop vegetables coarsely.
5. Place the asparagus and potato mixture on a bed of salad leaves.
6. Add vinaigrette or low calorie mayonnaise to taste.

This salad can be eaten on its own, with cold chicken or, as I prefer, with a smoked mackerel fillet. Mayonnaise goes very well with asparagus and potato but a simple vinaigrette is healthier and just as good. I suggest a mix of 4 to 1 of virgin olive oil and wine vinegar, but resist the temptation to use balsamic vinegar, which is too overpowering in this simple dish.

Chenin Blanc is again the white grape of choice for me but you might try a South African version as they are earthier and usually cheaper than those from the Loire.

Asparagus and eggs

Asparagus spears fit perfectly with buttery and creamy things but I think they go exceptionally well with eggs. The trick is to have plenty of steamed asparagus and just a little egg. A favourite Sunday night supper for my family is boiled (or scrambled) eggs with asparagus and brown bread. Real comfort food with the bread and asparagus used to mop up the egg. I know that eggs are not in the 'healthy food' category these days but, no matter your views, an occasional egg is not a cholesterol disaster.

An enjoyable supper for 2

12 asparagus spears
4 slices brown bread
2 large brown eggs
Seasoning

1. Cook the asparagus (see p.17), drain and leave to cool a little or if using asparagus from the can or jar, warm the spears.
2. Boil the eggs for 5 minutes, so they are still soft.
3. Crack the top off the eggs and eat, using the asparagus and bread as 'soldiers'.

I have suggested this dish as a supper but of course you can have it any time of day. If you substitute scrambled egg for the boiled and cook a few more asparagus spears, then the dish will make a fine lunch. It is just that I associate asparagus and eggs so strongly with a late night family meal. A nice cup of tea is the ideal drink, or even hot chocolate.

Aubergines

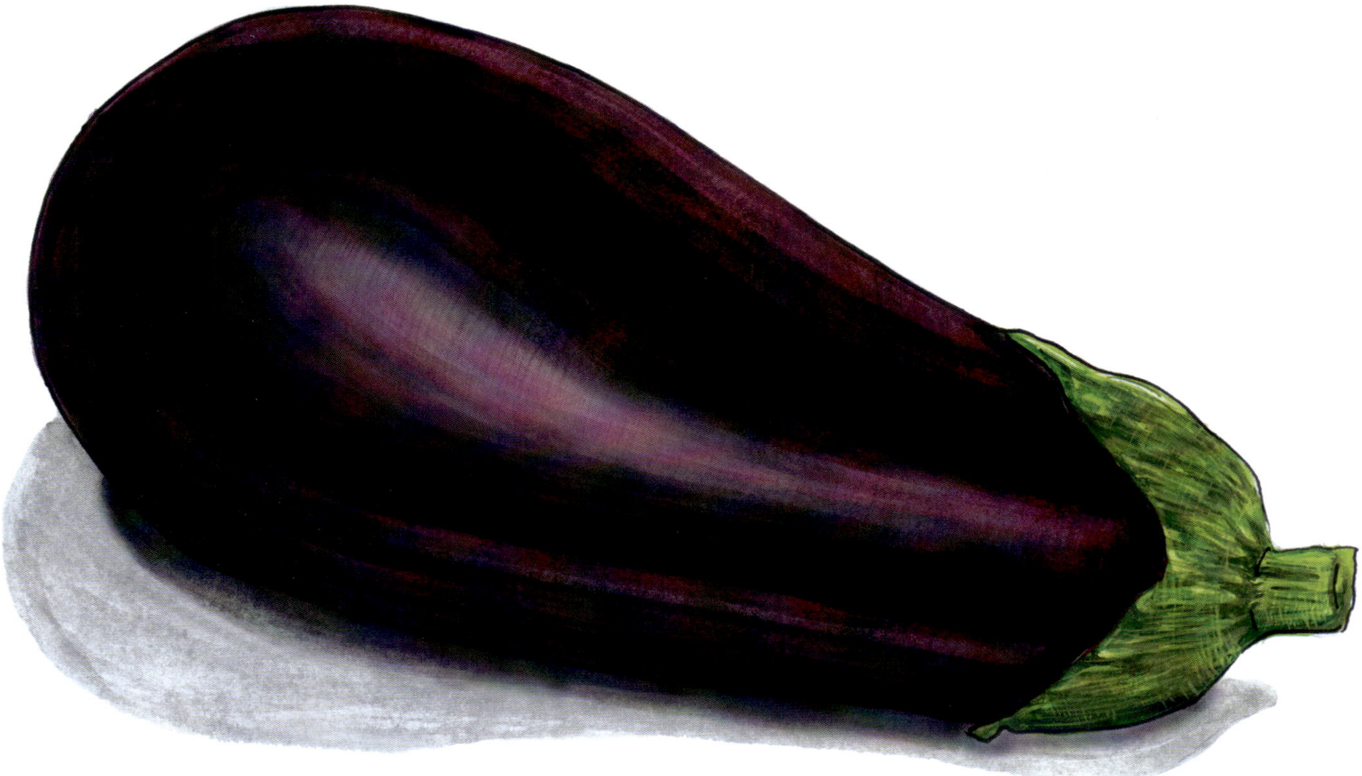

Aubergines

A lot of my friends cannot abide aubergines and many others have never eaten them. Even more just didn't know they have had and enjoyed them in Mediterranean dishes like ratatouille or moussaka. Dislike of aubergines may be because of their bitterness if not prepared correctly. You can peel the black skin off and then cube the flesh or, as I usually do, just cut the aubergine into slices, skin and all. At this point you must put the slices or cubes into a colander, salt the aubergine and leave for an hour with a heavy lid on top. Liquid will drain out and with it goes the bitterness! Aubergines are oily – they contain the fat-soluble vitamin E and carotenoids as well as some water-soluble vitamin C.

Ratatouille

This is a classic combination of aubergines, courgettes and tomatoes from Provence. As all of these are on our essential vegetable list it is a dish worth trying. My first visit to the Mediterranean was to the French city of Marseilles and my friends and I were determined to eat a local delicacy on our first night in this famous town. I was determined to try bouillabaisse, the fish soup, whereas the rest wanted ratatouille. At the end of the evening my friends were eulogising about the ratatouille but I was very quiet. My fish soup bit back and a large pointed bone had snagged in my lip. There was so much garlic and such in the soup that it irritated my wound resulting in a lower lip that was swollen to twice the normal size! How I wished I had gone along with the crowd and had taken the ratatouille. I ignored the jibes about my 'rubber lip' and kept silent. Ratatouille is packed with antioxidant colourful vegetables but I think aubergines dominate.

Serves 2 as a meal on its own or 4 as a side dish

2 medium sized aubergines
4 courgettes
450g (1lb) ripe tomatoes (skinned or not – cans are OK)
2 red peppers
2 large onions
2 garlic cloves
60ml (4tbsp) of virgin olive oil
Bunch of coriander (optional)
15ml (1tbsp) vinegar
Freshly ground black pepper
Pinch of sugar

1. Cube the aubergines and chop the courgettes into circles.
2. Place in colander with a sprinkling of salt for 1 hour, then dry off.
3. Chop the tomatoes coarsely and cut peppers into strips.
4. Chop the onions coarsely and chop the garlic finely.
5. Cook peppers, onions and garlic in oil until they soften a little – no more than 5 minutes in a deep pan.
6. Add the tomato, aubergines, courgettes, vinegar and sugar and cook for about 50 minutes with lid off.
7. Add the chopped coriander and boil off excess liquid over 5 minutes.
8. Finally, season with pepper; perhaps add a little sugar to taste.

Ratatouille is great either hot or cold. Try it on its own with lumps of fresh baguette or as a side dish with cold meats particularly ham. An intense full bodied red wine from the south of France goes well with this dish, such as Fitou or Corbière.

Stuffed aubergine

Aubergines are particularly suited to stuffing because of their shape and texture. You can stuff them with mince and rice or anything you like but I am going for a Turkish recipe named Imam Bayildi that I believe translates something like 'the priest has fainted'. The first dish I ever made with aubergines was Imam Bayildi and it happened to be for a dinner party. At this point I had never even tasted an aubergine – I had just seen a picture of the dish in a cookery book. I followed the recipe slavishly and avoided the obvious questions from my guests about what did Imam Bayildi taste like. Well nobody fainted but it was quite nice all the same, so ever since it has been something I like to make. I have simplified the preparation until it can be done more easily than the authentic recipe. I have also added and subtracted a few ingredients, so even the priest would no longer recognise it.

Serves 4

2 aubergines
225g (8oz) tomatoes
45ml (3tbsp) chopped flat leaf parsley
2 onions
2 cloves of garlic
15ml (1tbsp) virgin olive oil
½ a lemon
5ml (1tsp) of dill
50g (2oz) currants
10ml (2tsp) pine nuts
Salt and pepper

1. Cut the aubergines in half. Remove the seeds and central pulp.
2. Salt and leave upside down for 30 minutes to drain.
3. Brush off excess salt, cover with tin foil and bake in oven for 30 minutes at gas mark 6/200°C.
4. Chop tomatoes, parsley, onions and garlic. Fry onion and garlic in the olive oil until soft.
5. With a squeeze of lemon, mix together dill, currants, pine nuts tomatoes, parsley, onions and garlic into a stuffing and season.
6. Remove foil from aubergines. Add stuffing to the hollow centres.
7. Cover with the same foil and return to the oven for another 20 minutes.

Serve half an aubergine per person on a bed of lettuce leaves. I would drink a Greek white wine with this, but French Jurançon sec would be my favourite.

Aubergine pâté

Pâté can involve a lot of pluttering about and, although it is nice to eat it is not particularly good for you. Aubergine pâté is relatively easy and it is healthy.

Serves 2

1 large aubergine
45ml (3tbsp) of natural yogurt
30ml (2tbsp) of sunflower seeds
1 clove of garlic
1 lemon
Pepper
Few sprigs of fresh parsley, finely chopped

1. Slice the aubergine in half, salt and leave for 30 minutes to drain.
2. Brush the cut surfaces free of any salt and grill skin up on the. base of the grill pan for 20 minutes. The skin will be blackened. Let the aubergine cool in the grill pan.
3. Scoop out all the flesh into a blender; discard the blackened skin.
4. Add the yogurt, garlic clove, sunflower seeds and lemon juice to the aubergine pulp. Season with pepper and blitz in a blender.
5. Add the chopped parsley and serve as a dip.

Spread the aubergine pâté on biscuits or lumps of brown bread and enjoy. It is rather nice with a small glass of cold Madeira. Sticks of carrot or celery go well as dippers with the pâté.

Avocados

Avocados

Those of us over 50 will remember that in the 1960s avocado pear (as it always seemed to be called then) was this very popular but strange starter that competed with the more traditional shrimp cocktail or melon to begin every dinner party. Apart from dousing them with copious amounts of lemon juice no one really knew what to do with these wretched avocados did they? The stones were too perfect and round just to throw away and were such a struggle to get out of the unripe pear that people kept collections of them in their kitchens like trophies. A mound of mini cannon balls sitting on a plate – inevitably a curious child or tipsy adult would send them flying all over the floor!

They were not a great favourite of mine when I was younger but taste changes I guess, although it's probable that we have better recipes now. Avocados seem to have a new lease of life particularly with the increasing popularity of Mexican food (I have only just found out that avocados originated in Mexico). I no longer think of their texture being like toothpaste as I once did, but what do you think? They are certainly full of goodness and worth a revisit if you have not eaten them for a while and, if you eat them regularly, then keep up the good work!

Avocado is rich in minerals, antioxidants and high in vitamins so it is definitely healthy eye food. Try some of my favourite avocado recipes below.

Avocado starter

Here we go back to the 1960s! Well not quite if you make a vinaigrette rather than use lashings of lemon. If the avocados are hard, as they often are when you buy them, then do remember to leave them in the kitchen for a couple of days or so before eating. Then they will have some give in the skin when pressed with your fingers, otherwise they are not at all nice – a bit like the avocado bathroom suites that were once all the rage. When I lived in London in the 1970s and 1980s I moved around quite a lot and it seemed that each house I lived in had a new avocado bathroom suite.

Serves 4

2 avocados with some give in the skin
1 lemon or lime
120ml (8tbsp) virgin olive oil
30ml (2tbsp) balsamic vinegar (special occasions) or white wine vinegar
Pinch of pepper and salt
Pinch of sugar to taste

1. Split the avocados in half and remove the stone.
2. Squeeze the lemon but preferably lime juice over the avocados.
3. Make up the vinaigrette by mixing the oil, vinegar and seasoning in a small jug or pouring bowl.
4. I like to add a little sugar to taste but it is optional.
5. Fill the hole in each avocado half with the vinaigrette and enjoy with fresh buttered brown or wholemeal bread.

If you want to have wine, then dry whites are best with this starter and very cold Chablis is best of all for my taste. How about just a fizzy mineral water instead?

Guacamole

I have to say I love this stuff and to think that it is full of goodness as well is a great bonus. As with butcher's sausages and meat pies, there are many different combinations and special recipes. Buy the smooth stuff from the supermarket; it is fine. As an alternative I will give you a lazy coarse type that is just as nice. I think it is Californian rather than authentic Mexican but who cares. It tastes fine and is full of goodness. The fresh coriander alone gives plenty of lutein.

Serves 4 or more for a tea time snack, or double up for a barbecue

2 ripe avocados
1lime
4 medium tomatoes, chopped coarsely
1 large onion, finely chopped
2 fresh chillies or a pinch of chilli powder
75ml (5tbsp) fresh coriander
Pinch of salt and freshly ground black pepper

1. Peel the ripe avocados and remove the stone. Cut the flesh into cubes in a bowl. Squeeze in the juice of the lime.
2. Chop the tomatoes coarsely and add to the bowl with the chopped onion. (I don't bother to remove the tomato skins but you can if you prefer).
3. Remove the seeds from the chillies then slice them finely and fold in with the rest of the ingredients.

Use this mix immediately but, if you need to store it, do so in an airtight container in the fridge but not for too long because it gets watery. You don't have to add chilli if you don't like it and we often leave it out of this guacamole mixture. On the other hand coriander is an essential flavour but you can use dry powder if you haven't the fresh stuff. Eat the guacamole with tortilla chips, but hot pitta bread or ordinary toast is fine. The coarse guacamole mix is nice on the side of fresh salmon steaks. It goes well with any smoked fish including kippers. How about trying it with the sausages from the barbecue?

For drinks I think anything goes, but an ice cold Mexican lager is traditional. A dry white wine would be good, particularly a New Zealand Sauvignon Blanc.

Avocado milk shake

I know those of us in the AMD years are not in the milk shake years and I am not saying at all that this drink is good for you. I have put it here because it is a bit of fun and a different introduction to the avocado. I have heard that in some parts of the Far East Avocado ice cream is a hit but I will stop at this summer milk shake.

Serves 1 person in the USA, but for 2 elsewhere!

1 avocado
300ml (1/2 pint) of milk
30ml (2tbsp) of sugar
2 scoops of vanilla ice cream

1. Scoop the flesh out of an avocado.
2. Add the milk, sugar and ice cream.
3. Blend in a liquidiser.

Add loads of ice and drink on a warm summer's day. I had this first in the USA, hence the loads of ice cream and sugar. You can cut the quantities down a lot depending on taste and diet. The avocado, the milk and just a touch of sugar is fine.

Avocado and prawn sandwiches

To my mind you need white thick-sliced bread for this posh sandwich that became popular in the City of London in the 1980s as a lunch time special. If you can remember back this was the time of 'loads of money' satirised by Harry Enfield. You certainly needed loads of money to buy them in the new fangled sandwich bars. Along with BLTs (bacon, lettuce and tomato), chicken tikka salad and such like, avocado and prawn sandwiches were a little bit more interesting than the standard cheese and ham effort or the even more standard fried egg butty.

Sandwiches for 3

Wholemeal thick-sliced loaf
Butter or spread (optional)
1 ripe avocado
½ a lemon
90g (3oz) peeled prawns
15ml (1tbsp) low calorie mayonnaise

1. Put spread on slices of bread if required.
2. Peel and thinly slice the avocado; cover with lemon juice.
3. Place a few slices on the bread.
4. Mix the prawns with mayonnaise and pile on top of the avocado.
5. Cover each sandwich with another bread slice, then cut into 4.

Be generous with the filling. This recipe should make up to twelve quarters.

A nice glass of Spanish white Rioja would help wash the sandwich down, but mineral water and ice would be in keeping with the 1980s London theme.

Notes

Beans, Peas & Pulses

Beans, Peas & Pulses

Many foods have both good and bad features. Beans are an important source of protein and are rich in antioxidants but some beans, kidney beans for example, also have surface substances called lectins that can give you stomach ache. Fortunately these are soluble so it is recommended that both fresh and dry beans be soaked in cold water overnight before use. If you use canned beans they do not need soaking but a rinse is advisable. Remember dried beans need a lot of cooking, fresh beans much less but canned beans need relatively little, so being a lazy male I use canned beans as often as possible.

Broad bean stew

I have to say the poor old broad bean has been around for much of recorded history but it has had a very bad press in its time. Pythagoras, the ancient Greek with the theorem, hated them and gave out dire warnings about the dangers of this bean. In his own case he was absolutely right. The story goes that he was chased by a murderous mob who took exception to his teachings; he could have made good his escape, but needed to cross a field of broad beans and refused to do so and died at their hands. My mother made a huge pan of the stew using butter beans instead of broad beans every New Year's Eve (Hogmanay). My friends and I would go First Footing around various houses but end up at ours for bean stew or as they called it 'the thick soup with the big peas'!

Serves 4

500g (17oz) dried broad beans
12 thick rashers of bacon
1 good sized German garlic sausage or Spanish chorizo sausage
1 large onion
1 clove garlic
45ml (3tbsp) virgin olive oil
100ml (7tbsp) dry white sherry
300ml (1/2 pint) chicken stock
60ml (4tbsp) chopped fresh mint
5ml (1tsp) sugar
Paprika to taste

1. Soak the dried beans overnight in water – at least 12 hours.

2. Place the beans in fresh water in a large pan.
   Boil for 1hour, drain and then set aside.
3. Chop the bacon and sausage into bits and fry them in
   the oil in a casserole dish for 1 minute to seal.
4. Remove with a slotted spoon and fry the chopped
   onion and garlic in the oil and bacon juices for 3 minutes.
5. Add the beans and sauté them for 3 minutes.
6. Pour in the sherry and stock, add the meat plus
   the sugar and chopped mint.
7. Cook for 30 minutes and allow the liquid to reduce.
8. Shake on paprika to taste and serve in bowls.

This stew has a great flavour and thick slices of toast go well alongside this winter warmer. I like it so much that I would have it any time. I associate the stew with a small dram of Scots Whisky but a red wine from Southern France like Côtes du Roussillon Villages or a Californian Cabernet Sauvignon hits the spot.

Three bean salad

The USA is the land of the bean and I do think they have some superb recipes. Three bean salad is a standard and highly nutritious dish. It consists of kidney beans, chick peas and any another bean but I usually use haricot beans. I use small tins of each for speed but if you use packet beans please follow the instructions for soaking.

300g (11oz) tin of kidney beans
300g (11oz) tin of chick peas
300g (11oz) tin of cannellini beans
1 bunch spring onions
1 clove garlic
1 bunch fresh chives, chopped
1 bunch fresh coriander, chopped
1½ lemons
90ml (6tbsp) virgin olive oil
Pinch of sugar to taste
Salt and pepper

1. Wash the beans and chick peas and mix together in a bowl.
2. Chop the onion finely and crush the garlic clove.
3. Chop the chives and coriander coarsely and add the onion
   mixture and herbs to the bowl.

4. Squeeze in the lemon and add the oil; mix everything together.
5. Season and add some sugar if you like.
6. Keep cold in the fridge until needed.

It is so simple but my recipe might be too lemony for some of you. If so just use a single lemon or add more sugar. I make three bean salad on a regular basis to eat with cold rice, lettuce and chicken but the salad will go well with anything including fish and cold cuts. The lemon flavour means that the choice should be a dry white wine with acidity but not too much. Try an Australian Semillon or a Semillon blend.

Green beans and tomatoes

French green beans and plum tomatoes together make a very tasty and colourful mixture with the additional bonus of black olives to add to the taste and texture. It is also high on the healthy list being rich in antioxidants.

Serves 2 well (and probably enough for 4)

15ml (1tbsp) virgin olive oil
1 onion, chopped
1 clove garlic, sliced
6 plum tomatoes
150ml (¼ pint) white wine
450g (1lb) green beans
1 lemon
12 stoned black olives

1. Warm the oil in a large pan and add the onions and garlic, softening them over 3 minutes.
2. Chop the tomatoes roughly (remove the skins in warm water previously if you wish but I don't bother).
3. Top and tail the French green beans and split length ways.
4. Squeeze the lemon into the pan and add the wine.
5. Mix in the beans, tomatoes and olives. Simmer for 20 minutes.
6. Once the juices have reduced, season and serve.

The bean and tomato mix is a nice lunch but an even better supper that reminds me of holidays whether they be in Cartagena or Cleethorpes. Enjoy the remains of a French white Vin de Table – the rest of it went into the recipe!

Lentils and rice

Lentils I associate with old fashioned soups on the one hand and tasteless vegetarian dishes on the other. As a vegetable the lentil need not be condemned to being some kind of medicine that is good for you but with no real quality taste. To prove my point I include an old favourite recipe. This lentil and rice dish is a simple stew that has a bit of everything including flavour and antioxidants for the eye.

A hearty meal for 2 (and enough for 4)

60g (2oz) basmati rice
250g (8oz) red lentils
60g (2oz) green beans
1 red sweet pepper
1 large leek
120g (4oz) broccoli florets
2 pints of chicken stock
1 tin chopped tomatoes
2 garlic cloves
5ml (1tsp) chilli powder
5ml (1tsp) ground cumin
15ml (1tbsp) fresh basil
Seasoning to taste

1. Cook the rice and lentils for 20 minutes in the chicken stock in a large pot.
2. Chop up the beans, pepper and leek and trim the broccoli to florets.
3. Add these vegetables and everything else to the pot apart from the basil and simmer for at least 15 minutes.
4. Add the chopped basil and season just before serving.

The essential thing here is the rice and lentils that give this vegetable hot pot a risotto texture. Apart from the tin of tomatoes, you can use any other vegetables you fancy – cauliflower, carrots, asparagus and cabbage all work well in this healthy stew. Lentils and wine don't really go so I would just have a flavoured mineral water with this, or how about a fruit smoothie?

Peas and lettuce

This recipe mixes fresh peas with small lettuces and I think it brings the best out of both. Peas have some lutein as does lettuce. They both have beta carotene, vitamin C and some iron. Peas have other minerals including zinc and they are a protein source.

Serves 4 as a side dish

1 medium onion
15ml (1tbsp) virgin olive oil
2 midget gem lettuces
450g (1lb) of fresh garden peas
5ml (1tsp) dried mixed herbs
Pinch of sugar to taste

1. Chop the onion as fine as possible. Fry in the oil for 2 minutes.
2. Chop up the lettuces and place in the pan with the shelled peas.
3. Add the mixed herbs.
4. Cover with a little water, place a lid on the pan and cook for 20 minutes.
5. Add sugar to taste.

During the cooking, the dish may need additional water so check the vegetables during the 20 minutes. The vegetables should not be drowned!

A light Italian red is fine with this dish or perhaps try a Valpollicella?

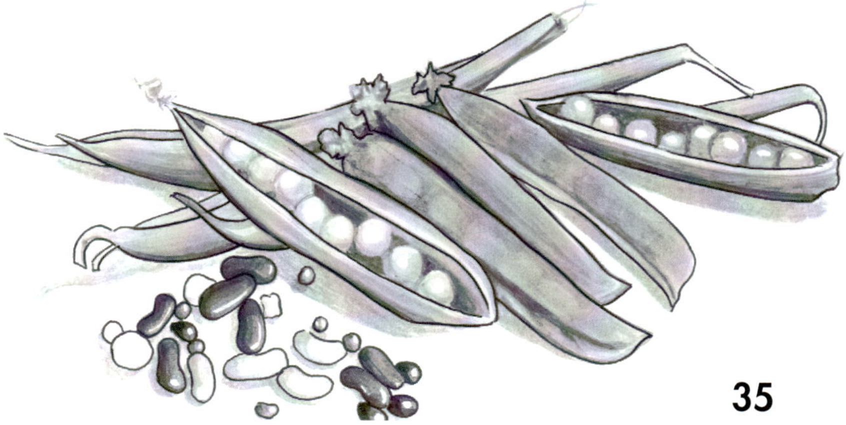

Beetroot

Beetroot

Scotland, where I was brought up as a boy, was not renowned for its beetroot. They would appear in the greengrocers all right but no one knew what to do with them apart from pickling in vinegar. My Mum on the other hand was a Londoner and 'civilised' and that meant, among many other things, that she had a host of recipes for fresh beetroot and didn't much care for the pickled stuff. Only my Mum could think that a cornerstone of civilisation was what you did with a beetroot. I don't think our neighbours thought Mum was a snob, only 'colourful'. Her hands certainly were colourful after a day boiling up fresh beets from the grocer or more usually from our garden.

Beetroot is back and it is enjoying a revival so the pundits are saying. For my part I never knew it had any popularity to begin with. Now it seems that we have to consider the humble and obscure beetroot as a 'power food' from a 'vitality plant' with wondrous properties. It makes me think that someone has too many beets to get rid of? Beetroot may not be a wonder plant but it is a healthy one unless like me you cannot resist covering hot beets with lashings of butter. Beetroot has betacarotene, vitamin C and zinc from the eye point of view, but also a host of other goodies for general health so at least some of its recent good press is justified.

Fresh beetroot sandwiches

If you have not prepared fresh beetroot before then the standard way is to boil them in your oldest pot (the beetroot stains both pot and you) like my Mum would do. For me boiling is too messy, I buy them cooked and vacuum packed from the supermarket. If you want to go ahead and do the boiling thing, then stuff them straight into the pan. Do not try to peel them or cut the tops right off (twist the tops off a little only) and this minimises the mess. Cook for about an hour but you know the beets are ready when the skin slides off to the touch; a pair of rubber gloves might be a useful investment. Microwaving on full power will reduce the cooking down to 10 minutes; remember to turn them over at 5 minutes.

Sandwiches for 4

4 medium sized cooked beetroots
8 slices of your favourite bread
Butter or spread
Light mayonnaise
Pinch of pepper

1. Top and tail the beetroot and peel off the skin while still warm but not hot.
2. If you have the supermarket vacuum packet, then warm them in the microwave.
3. Thick slice the beets using one per sandwich.
4. Place on a buttered slice of bread; add a sprinkle of pepper.
5. Spread the mayo on the other slice – not too much – cut and eat.

The beetroot can be cold or warm but I find warm beetroot sandwiches to be a comfort food that reminds me of childhood – watch out for red lips! The books say an unoaked dry white wine goes best with beetroot like a Soave from Italy for instance. I would choose a light red (remember the phenols are supposed to be good for you if you drink one glass every leap year or something like that).

Beetroot salad

The boring beetroot has two close friends that bring the best out of it. One is the green apple and the other is the walnut. Put the three of them together and you really do have a special salad mix. It is an exceptionally health conscious mixture as well as tasting, to my way of thinking, exquisite.

4 boiled beetroots
2 green apples
1 red salad onion
100g (4oz) or 1 small bag peeled walnuts
60ml (4tbsp) virgin olive oil
15ml (1tbsp) balsamic vinegar

1. Chop up the beetroot and apple (peeling the apples is optional) and place in a salad bowl.
2. Cut the onion into thin rings and mix with the rest.
3. Crush the walnuts in the bag, but only a little.

4. Make the vinaigrette by mixing the oil and vinegar.
5. Add the nuts and vinaigrette to the salad.

If you do not find the vinaigrette to your liking then low calorie mayonnaise is a sound alternative dressing. The creamy texture of the mayonnaise and the fibrous beetroot are a perfect blend. A French stick cut roughly would be nice with this salad. If you have a little olive oil left over, rub it with some crushed garlic into the bread. The meat eaters can choose any cold meats to go with the salad, but I like robust tastes, for example salami or pastrami. Pickled herring is possibly the best partner of all. Most wines are dull with the beetroot salad but a rough red wine such as Bulls Blood from Hungary is fine.

Notes

Broccoli

Broccoli

Who actually likes broccoli? Be honest now – there are those who eat broccoli and those who don't, but there aren't too many who relish this vegetable, are there? Some think it healthy or fashionable to eat raw florets with a dip but, at a party, when all the cheese straws, carrot batons and even the celery have been dipped into extinction, there is always a great pile of raw broccoli left. As well as having masses of healthy antioxidant vitamins, it also contains a number of anticancer agents. So much so that the Americans are making a broccoli pill to concentrate broccoli's goodness and avoid eating the real thing. Guess what? The pill is bright green!

I don't mind cooked broccoli but my wife finds it tough going particularly the stalks. I say to her 'eat up the stalks they are good for you!' and embarrass her into eating some. Of course they are good; they are full of iron, some calcium and plenty of other minerals. A touch of zinc for the eyes is present plus plenty of lutein, vitamin C and loads of antioxidants. On the other hand, Dee's health is only part of the reason for my bullying – mostly I want a laugh at her expense. Anything she doesn't like gets shoved into her cheek, which then swells like a hamster's. Numerous faces get pulled, the stalk flies rapidly from one cheek to the other and at last the offending item is washed away by a large gulp of water. Triumph! Then I get the steely look so that my grin fades rapidly with the realisation that she will get her own back. Dry lamb chops (not a favourite) and celery soup (ugh!) will be on our menu soon.

Broccoli and Stilton soup

My Mum just loves this soup, as do I. It is a treat for us and can be made with any of the smelly cheeses like Danish Blue, but I think Stilton is the best.

Enough for a few hungry people or lots if you are prepared to share!

60ml (4tbsp) olive oil
225g (8oz) chopped onion
1 litre (1¾ pints) chicken stock (fresh or made with cubes)

1 medium sized head of broccoli
Freshly ground black pepper
25g (1oz) plain flour
50g (2oz) Stilton cheese
Sprig of parsley to serve

1. Take half the olive oil and fry the chopped onions in a large pan then add the stock and bring it all to the boil;
2. Break up the broccoli and add to the pan. Pepper well.
3. Cook the broccoli for at least 15 minutes, leave to cool and then liquidise until smooth.
4. Heat the remaining oil in the pan and add the flour and cook gently for a few moments; then add back the broccoli and boil for 3 minutes.
5. Add the cheese a little at a time until it is all dissolved.
6. Serve in small bowls with a sprig of parsley on top.

Acidic wines do not go all that well with this soup, but try a nice little glass of Ruby Port, or even a Marsala from Italy.

Broccoli and cheese bake

Everyone knows cauliflower and cheese because it is an old classic. Broccoli is a little more nutritious than cauliflower and certainly is far richer in antioxidants and minerals. It is a fair substitute in a cheese bake and certainly it is more colourful. All I have done to this family recipe is substitute broccoli for cauliflower but it is not quite the same ideal combination (you could always try half broccoli and half cauliflower?). At my home in Scotland the cauliflower version was a winter standby. There was no heating in our kitchen but the cauliflower and cheese, straight out of the oven, was like a furnace. The foolish and greedy would not use it for hand warming but immediately try to eat it. A bad mistake: the roof of the mouth would be assaulted by cheese the same temperature as molten lava! It is not the same dish eaten warm as it is hot! To make it a little more interesting, I've made it into a pie.

Serves 2 as a main meal on its own (or 4 if served with boiled potatoes, in their skins of course)

1kg (2¼ lb) broccoli
1 medium onion
50g (2oz) butter
25g (1oz) plain flour
300ml (½ pt) milk
10ml (2tsp) Dijon or whole grain mustard
50g (2oz) grated cheese
Pepper to taste
45ml (3tbsp) single cream
350g (12oz) packet of puff pastry

1. Chop up the broccoli and blanch in boiling water then drain.
2. Chop and fry onion in the butter for 3 minutes.
3. Add the flour and cook it through.
4. Remove from the heat and stir in the milk.
5. Add the mustard and all of the grated cheese. Cook and stir until the sauce thickens. Add pepper – be generous.
6. Finally add the cream and the blanched broccoli stirring well.
7. Place the contents into a pie dish; cover with the rolled out pastry and make a hole in the middle for the steam to escape.
8. Bake at gas mark 6/200°C for 25 minutes then serve immediately.

A Spanish red wine such as Rioja or a Portuguese red like Dão would be my choice with this dish. Most reds are OK but I don't think whites work at all well.

Broccoli, tuna and pasta

I think that broccoli works well with pasta and also with oily fish like tuna. In this dish there is the healthy combination of broccoli and red peppers for antioxidants and minerals, fish for omega-3 fatty acids, and a bit of bulk from the pasta helps to fill you up when hungry.

Dee calls this type of food a 'flat dinner' meaning a meal you can rustle up quickly. This type of food she associates with her time living in a flat when everyone was rushing here, there and everywhere with little time for cooking. As for me I thought she meant it was flat on the plate! As for this flat dinner, it is ideal for busy people and can be made the day before.

Serves 4–6 depending on the size of their appetites (or if there are less than 4, put some in the freezer)

350 g (12oz) pasta shells
350 g (12oz) broccoli florets
1 medium sized red pepper, chopped
10ml (2tsp) capers
2 cloves garlic
5ml (1tsp) oregano
45ml (3tbsp) virgin olive oil
30ml (2tbsp) red wine vinegar
Freshly ground black pepper
1 small 175g (6oz) tin of tuna
25g (1oz) fresh basil leaves
50g (2oz) grated Parmesan or your favourite cheese

1. Cook pasta in salted boiling water for 1 minute less than on the packet instructions. Drain and set on one side.
2. Blanch broccoli florets and chopped red peppers in boiling water for no more than 3–4 minutes.
3. Make the dressing by combining the capers, crushed garlic, oregano, oil and red wine vinegar in a small mixing bowl; add some pepper.
4. Combine the pasta, broccoli, red pepper and tuna; add the dressing.
5. Place mixture in ovenproof bowl and top it off with the grated cheese and shredded basil.
6. Bake in the oven at gas mark 6/200°C for 15 minutes.
7. Serve straight from the oven or it can be eaten cold or reheated in the microwave the next day.

Most white wines (or rosé) go with this dish. Try Muscadet-sur-lit from the Loire Valley.

Saucy broccoli florets

Broccoli is not everyone's favourite vegetable, especially if it is just boiled and nothing else done to it. There are a number of sauces and marinades that make broccoli more interesting. Here is one that I like.

Serves 4 generously as the vegetable portion of a main meal

450g (1lb) fresh or frozen broccoli florets
15ml (1tbsp) sesame seeds
15ml (1tbsp) vegetable oil
15ml (1tbsp) red wine vinegar
15ml (1tbsp) soy sauce
10ml (2tsp) of sugar

1. Cook the broccoli in boiling salted water for 15 minutes. Drain and arrange florets in a serving dish.
2. Toast the sesame seeds on a tray under the grill for a few minutes.
3. Add the seeds and all the other ingredients to a small pan and heat up to boiling.
4. Pour over the broccoli making sure all the florets are coated, then serve straight away.

I like the taste of sesame seeds but poppy or even mustard seeds will do the job. Sesame seeds are best known for topping hamburger buns, but they are a good source of vitamin B and from an eye point of view, vitamins C and E are also present. Have the broccoli dish with any roast or stew.

The choice of wine would depend on the meat dish but if you are being good and having lots of broccoli and a generous coating of sesame and soy sauce, then a Beaujolais Villages from the Rhône would be nice.

Brussels Sprouts

Brussels Sprouts

Brussels sprouts are nowhere close to being my favourite vegetable to the extent that I can manage a couple of boiled brussels with my Christmas turkey, but that's it for the straightforward boiled ones. On the other hand, I do enjoy trying to make them into a palatable dish, principally because they are very good for you, being packed with essential minerals and antioxidants. I have to say that I find them bitter, and most of what I do is to mask the bitterness and try to use partners that bring the best out in them. I know people who just love boiled brussels sprouts and can't get enough of them. All I can do is watch on in admiration, and leave a small pile of them on the side of my plate.

Bubble and squeak

Any cooked greens and left over mashed potato provide the basics for bubble and squeak, but I think the very best greens for this job has to be brussels sprouts. I try to avoid the boiled brussels on Christmas Day, but the cold leftovers on Boxing Day are mine!

Serves 4–6 (depending how hungry you are)

450g (1lb) leftover brussels sprouts
1kg (2¼ lb) mashed potatoes
15ml (1tbsp) milk
60ml (4tbsp) virgin olive oil
Salt and pepper
Plain flour as required
Nob of butter

1. Chop the sprouts up roughly.
2. Mix the sprouts, potatoes and milk together with half the olive oil and season well.
3. Take four fist-sized lumps of mixture and flatten by hand on a floured chopping board.
4. Cook one at a time in an oiled non-stick frying pan and add a sliver of butter at the end to give colour.

Bubble and squeak works because of the contrast in flavour, texture and colour and although I have labelled it as an after Christmas Day treat of course it can be eaten at any time you have some spare mash and sprouts.

Traditionally bubble and squeak is cooked in lard and loads of butter but it does not have to be so unhealthy, and I actually prefer it when cooked in olive oil. While the bubble and squeak is being prepared I have some rashers of lean back bacon on the grill and garden peas (frozen, canned or fresh) heating in a small pan. Together they make a lovely and filling meal that is very tasty, especially with a little chutney or piccalilli on the side. My wife Dee likes to have a glass of milk, but I think a glass of dry cider is excellent accompaniment.

Sprouts and chestnuts

When we have roast turkey or chicken, whatever the time of year, brussels sprouts are never too far away. As I have said, they are not to my taste, but I have my ways of trying to get the best out of them and one way is to mix them with chestnuts. The two work well together in texture and flavour. Chestnuts are a great source of vitamin C.

Serves 2 large or 4 small appetites

450g (1lb) brussels sprouts
A ½ tin (4oz) water chestnuts
15ml (1tbsp) butter substitute or oil
Bunch of fresh parsley
Grating of nutmeg to taste
5ml (1tsp) of sugar

1. Bring salted water to the boil add chopped parsley and the sprouts and cook for 20 minutes and drain.
2. Add butter to a large pot plus the chopped chestnut fragments, the sugar and heat.
3. Add the sprouts and heat through.
4. Serve immediately with a little ground nutmeg.

Butter goes well with this vegetable, but substitutes are fine. It is important to be aware of cholesterol, but remember a little fat dramatically increases your ability to absorb the fat-soluble vitamins and carotenes.

A lighter red wine would be my choice such as a New Zealand Pinot Noir.

Brussels sprouts and oranges

Another simple recipe that makes a remarkable difference to sprouts and it has the additional bonus of vitamin C from the oranges.

Serves 4 (or 2 enthusiasts)

450g (1lb) sprouts
30ml (2tbsp) butter (or olive oil)
2 large oranges
Lots of freshly ground black pepper

1. Boil the sprouts in salted water for 20 minutes then drain.
2. Heat the butter and cook the sprouts for 2 minutes.
3. Peel and add the orange segments; cook for another 1–2 minutes.
4. Serve, well peppered.

There is enough here for four portions and the dish goes well with braised liver and baked potato. Roast chicken is fine but turkey and duck are far better. A Californian or Chilean Merlot is a reasonable wine with this orange and brussels sprout mix.

Notes

Cabbages & Greens

Cabbages and Greens

'It was the best of veg and the worst of veg' to paraphrase dreadfully the opening line from 'A Tale of Two Cities' by Charles Dickens. I think cabbage can be great when done well but doesn't it really hit an all time vegetable low when in the hands of an office canteen cook? Have any of you had the bitter experience of trying to eat hospital cabbage? The Liverpool Royal University Hospital is fine exponent of the culinary destruction of this important vegetable. In my school on school dinner days, I have this abiding memory of lumpy mash partly separating greasy lamb stew and watery cabbage. A colourful rainbow would form where the fat of the lamb met the water of the cabbage gloop. Totally inedible, but it was a science project on my plate.

Yet the cabbage is full of goodness but, if it is overcooked then all the healthy things are in the green water that goes down the sink. My granny always kept the cabbage water to thin gravy, and Dee my wife remembers as a child at home in Ireland, lining up to drink the cabbage water. So our parents knew a thing or two after all! What are all the goodies then?

The greenest of cabbage, those like kale, savoy and winter greens, have the highest content of lutein of all vegetables. It has to be said that all types of cabbage have very respectable levels of lutein. I'm often asked, if lutein is a yellow dye, why are cabbages green? It is because the green dye chlorophyll masks the lutein's yellow, but when the cabbage gets old, the green is oxidised and then the yellow shows through. Kale and savoy are also rich in vitamin A as is the Chinese cabbage called bokchoi. Respectable amounts of vitamin C are present in all cabbage types but particularly the bitter red cabbage and bokchoi. Even canned sauerkraut has a reasonable amount. Minerals abound in all cabbages, so get stuck in!

Remember, eating more cabbage need not involve complicated recipes. Cook up a load of Savoy cabbage for dinner and there will be plenty left to make bubble and squeak. Extra spoonfulls of pickled red cabbage on lamb stew or what in Liverpool is called 'scouse' will give you antioxidants, and winter greens with any brown stew is a nice treat.

Caldo verde

I hope that is the right spelling! It is a Portuguese green soup made from cabbage. Dee and I were in Oporto one spring and we were starving one lunch time. We followed some workmen into a back street café and ordered their standard set lunch (typical Brits, we couldn't cope with a foreign menu). However, we knew our limitations: the day before, we had tried to order a glass of white wine in some place where there was no English spoken and ended up with beers plus a ham and cheese toastie! As it turned out, the set lunch was a banquet for less than £5 each and that's not bad for a Scotsman like myself. Neither Dee nor I ever forgot the Portuguese green soup that started this great meal off; it was exceptional. Dee has her own version of this Portuguese classic and here it is.

Serves 3–4

1 large or 2 small onions
15ml (1tbsp) virgin olive oil
1 or 2 cloves garlic depending on taste
1 cabbage preferably a loose, dark leafed variety (spring or winter greens), sliced
600ml to 1 litre (1–1¾ pints) chicken stock
1 large potato (a floury one is best), cubed
Salt and pepper to taste

1. Slice onion and fry gently in the oil, adding chopped garlic at the same time.
2. After 1 minute, add the cabbage and gently fry to soften for 10 minutes – do not burn or brown.
3. Add the chicken stock with the potato and bring to the boil; simmer gently until the potato is soft.
4. Blend completely or, for a more authentic texture, ease off to leave plenty of bits. Season to taste. Eat greedily with lumps of crusty bread.

Any dry white wine is fine with the soup but a Portuguese white is particularly appropriate so try a Vinho Verde.

Mother-in law's bacon and cabbage

My wife Dee is Irish so we go often to the Emerald Isle by car and ferry. We have an early start and usually arrive in Dublin famished. Dublin's not the easiest city to get through but eventually we reach the countryside. Our routine is to stop at the same hotel and we get there just as the lunchtime service is in full swing. The hotel prides itself on its extensive menu, but I'm not bothered – there is only one thing for me and that is bacon and cabbage with lashings of flowery potatoes. Who would reach for caviar when there is bacon and cabbage to be had?

Serves 4

A large piece of back bacon is best – usually available from the butcher about 4 or 5 inches thick
12 cloves
2 or more bay leaves
2 cone heart cabbages or 1 very large savoy cabbage
12 floury potatoes
12 carrots
White sauce – standard packet

1. Score the skin on the bacon; insert several cloves and place a couple of bay leaves under the string.
2. Put the bacon into a pressure cooker and just cover with water. Put on to cook, and when pressure is reached, turn down for 40 minutes.
3. Meanwhile prepare cabbage by washing and slicing. Set aside.
4. Prepare and cook potatoes. It is best, if they are nice and floury, to boil them in their jackets and eat them that way!
5. When the bacon is cooked, remove and let rest.
6. Cook the cabbage in the bacon water for 10 minutes or so. A little bread soda, the tip of a knife's worth, in the water helps the cabbage keep its colour.
7. If you are feeling very hungry, slice up some carrots and boil till tender.
8. Lashings of butter traditionally serve as the only sauce but a packet of white sauce mix might be healthier.

9. Just before all the vegetables are ready, remove the skin from bacon and slice longways – like a rasher and serve. Enjoy!

Drink Guinness for the iron content or a Spanish white from Penedes like Vina Sol.

Braised red cabbage

When I first worked abroad it was only for a few weeks in southern Germany at a place called Wurzburg on the River Main. German food is OK for the most part, but sometimes it can get tough when they go too traditional. I went for dinner with some people I worked with and we were served boiled white sausage, dough balls (not at all like our dumplings) and red cabbage. I just couldn't cope with the first two but the cabbage was spectacular. I've an old recipe that is something close – do try it! This red cabbage dish does indeed go well with sausages (not the white ones, but they do need to have some flavour. Butcher's best or even Frankfurters will be fine).

Serves 6

1 medium sized red cabbage
Salt and pepper
1 sliced onion
45ml (3tbsp) butter (or olive oil)
30ml (2tbsp) vinegar
30ml (2tbsp) red wine (cheap and nasty is best)
2 green cooking apples
Cornflour (optional)
30ml (2tbsp) brown sugar
10 ml (2tsp) redcurrant (or any) jelly
Pinch of cloves, nutmeg and pepper

1. Wash and shred the cabbage and sprinkle with salt and pepper.
2. Cook the onion in the butter or oil for about a minute, then add the cabbage, vinegar and all the wine. I use my father in law's home brew that, if kept in your mouth too long, dissolves the fillings!
3. Cover and cook on low heat for 10 minutes stirring now and then.

4. Peel, core and slice the apples and add to the mixture with the cloves, nutmeg and sugar. Simmer for 30 minutes or until the cabbage and apples are tender.
5. Finally stir in the jelly and add enough cornflour to thicken the sauce if wanted.
6. Eat with nice sausages and boiled potatoes.

Wine? Try anything German (Piesporter is inexpensive and appropriate). German wines work well with the cabbage and apple combination.

Healthy kale stew

My eldest two boys, Richard and Matthew, are both vegetarian but that does not mean they eat well. Richard is the worst; he thinks that beans on organic toast is a banquet. When I get them home, which is not often these days, I try to feed them up with an emphasis on nutritious bowls of vegetable stew. This recipe is right at the top of the list for eye health given that the central ingredients are kale (lutein and antioxidants in abundance), a very green leafy vegetable, and carrots (vitamin A and beta carotene). It does not taste too bad either; particularly on a cold evening when something piping hot is in order.

Kale can be hard to get, so use winter or spring greens instead if you have to. Remember kale and dark greens are cheap, so go against your natural thrift and waste the coarser leaves that can be too strong or even bitter.

Serves 4 hungry lads or 6 normal folks (and all will get a goodly supply of lutein)

450g (1lb) carrots
350g (12oz) parsnips
1 large onion
15ml (1tbsp) olive oil
1 or 2 large kale
60ml (4tbsp) water
30ml (2tbsp) dark soya sauce

1. Chop the carrots and parsnips into rings; dice the onion roughly.
2. In a deep frying pan, add the oil and sauté first the carrots and parsnips; add the onion after 2 minutes. Keep going until the vegetables are becoming tender.

3. Meanwhile chop up the youngest kale leaves after removing the stems. Lightly steam for no more than 5 minutes.
4. Lightly oil a casserole dish; add the kale and the rest of the vegetables.
5. Mix the water and soya sauce and add to the dish.
6. Cover and cook the stew for 15 minutes at gas mark 6/200°C.

Eat this stew while hot with crusty bread. Confirmed meat eaters might wish to poach some smoked golden cutlets to go with this and that would be a healthy option, although grilled lamb chops or braised liver would be my first choice.This dish needs a red wine with some body such as the popular Italian red Valpolicella.

Dolmas of greens

Any of you who have been to a Greek restaurant or to Greece on holiday might have tried dolmas that are basically vine leaf parcels filled with chopped bits and pieces. Substitute nutritious cabbage for vine leaves; these parcels also contain nuts, seeds and cheese rich in fat-soluble vitamins, also apple, lemon and raisins rich in vitamin C, and vegetables full of antioxidants.

Makes about 8–10 parcels (enough for about 4 or 5 people.

1 large green cabbage (or any cabbage with firm leaves)
1 large onion
1 clove garlic
1 stick celery
1 carrot
50g (2oz) walnuts
50g (2oz) sunflower seeds
60ml (4tbsp) of olive oil
225g (8oz) apple, chopped
50g (2oz) raisins
30ml (2tbsp) of lemon juice
15ml (1tbsp) of honey
15ml (1tbsp) of dark soy sauce
225g (8oz) ricotta cheese
A little butter

1. Select firm large cabbage leaves and set aside the rest. Cut the thick stems out.
2. Boil the cabbage leaves for 3 minutes.
3. Chop up the vegetables and walnuts.
4. Fry the onion, crushed garlic, celery, carrots, walnuts and sunflower seeds in olive oil until cooked.
5. Add the chopped apples, raisins, cheese, lemon juice, honey, and soy sauce to the hot mix; season to taste.
6. Add a scoop of mixture to each cabbage leaf and roll up folding in the edges.
7. Butter a baking tray, place the parcels on and cover with foil.
8. Place in a preheated oven at gas mark 3/160°C for 25 minutes.

Serve hot from the oven. Two per person is a nice starter or supper dish. As a main meal, serve them with boiled new potatoes and a little butter.

Drink a Greek wine such as Domestica with dolmas; most Greek or Cypriot wines do the business, although not the famous retsina which I find overpowers many foods.

Notes

Carrots

Carrots

If you search the internet you can find some pretty wild claims about the boring old carrot. The carrot is being called the 'vision veg' and 'sight saver' and such like silly names that wildly exaggerate its importance. Of course we know on health grounds that the carrot is a fabulous source of beta carotene. It does seem that the humble carrot has made a comeback at least with the health lobby. Recommending plenty of carrots is being bandied about now almost as much as it was in the early years of World War II when eating your way through a fortuitous carrot glut was seen as a way of avoiding night blindness. The carrot deserves its good press because, as well as being a superb source of beta carotene, it is also a source of folic acid, B vitamins and iron. In addition, from the eye health point of view, the carrot has vitamins C and E.

Carrot salad

Fresh young carrots are best but any carrot will do. The main items are carrots and currants which together bring a lovely sweetness to the dish that is offset by lemon juice.

Serves 4 generously

450g (1lb) of young carrots
140 g (5oz) currants
½ a lemon
30ml (2tbsp) sunflower oil
5ml (1tsp) sesame oil
15ml (1tbsp) brown sugar
5ml (1tsp) fresh oregano
Salt and pepper

1. Grate all the carrot finely and add to a salad bowl.
2. Mix in the currants.
3. Rind the half lemon and extract the juice.
4. Add the lemon, oils and sugar to the grated carrot and mix.
5. Sprinkle on the oregano and season.

This is a nice light meal on its own, or put it with cheese or other salads. Try unoaked white wines like Côtes de Gascogne.

Carrot mash and spinach

We as a Scots/Irish family can't resist beating everything into mash. Not just potatoes and swedes get pulverised – it is also peas, parsnips, cabbage, marrow and frequently the poor old carrot. If we hear banging and thumping going on in our kitchen, then we know we are just about to eat. Each vegetable meets its end with a different implement; for example, peas get smashed with a big spoon, potatoes succumb to the traditional masher, and cabbage gets done in with the side of a plate. Dee loves mashed carrot and I like to put it with spinach. In terms of eye health, antioxidant vitamins, minerals, lutein and beta carotene, this combination is hard to beat, but just to go over the top we have lemon juice, basil and almonds as extras.

450g (1lb) carrots
225g (½ lb) packet of baby spinach leaves
½ lemon
Seasoning
15ml (1tbsp) almond flakes
45ml (3tbsp) torn fresh basil leaves

1. Wash, top and tail the carrots, and then slice them into rings. Add the rings to salted boiling water and cook for up to 10 minutes.
2. Spread the spinach leaves over the base of an oven proof serving dish and squeeze on lemon juice.
3. Mash the cooked carrot, season well with black pepper and scoop onto the spinach.
4. Spread over the torn basil leaves and sprinkle on the almond flakes.
5. Place in a low oven until needed.

The spinach will wilt enough with the heat of the carrot and then a bit more in the low oven. The young leaves certainly do not need much cooking unless that is to your own taste. The mixture is fine on its own, as part of a vegetarian, meal or it will accompany a range of roast meats. It goes well with oily fish like mackerel or even simple fishcakes. How about grilling some fishcakes and putting them with mashed potato and a nice big helping of carrot mash and spinach? Go on, I'm sure you would like it with a nice glass of Bourgogne Aligoté.

Carrot batons in courgette rings

I know that further education at our Nation's night schools is a great thing but there are minuses as well as pluses. On the dos and don'ts of night classes, I have only two important pieces of advice. Do not go to wine appreciation classes because they are extremely expensive. I became an enthusiastic wine buff on the basis of attending a few wine classes. I do not have talent in wine appreciation, but I now have expensive tastes. If, at a supermarket, you are happy with the stuff on the bottom shelf don't educate your palate to the stuff on the top shelf – just look at the price difference! In addition to wrecking the family so-called food bill, I have also become the family bore by banging on about 'up and coming New World wines', 'changing styles in French wine making' and worst of all, "When can we go on a wine tasting holiday?"

The plus was convincing my wife, who is a good cook anyway, to go to cookery classes at night school. She left all the failures (of which there were very few) in the school dustbins, but brought all the successes home for me to enjoy and be washed down, of course, by a couple of glasses of overpriced wine. Dee was convinced then and remains convinced that meals don't need to be complicated – a little effort in presentation can make all the difference. The following carrot dish is one of hers from those times that we still enjoy.

Serves 4

450g (1lb) carrots 2 large courgettes Salt and pepper

1. Wash and chop the carrots into batons of equal length.
2. Chop the courgettes into rings between 1 and 2 cm thick.
3. Remove the core of the rings with a pointed kitchen knife.
4. Stuff the carrot batons through the rings until they are packed full.
5. Put the rings into boiling salted water with a large slotted spoon and cook for little more than 5 minutes. Drain and season.

The red batons in the green rings look very nice as well as being good for you. The hardest part is cutting the carrot batons and I know when Dee makes the dish now she cheats and buys the carrot batons ready made from the supermarket. Well why not?

Cauliflower

Cauliflower

Overcooking has done nothing for this vegetable's reputation; which of us has not had cauliflower mush served up at various times? At the other extreme raw cauliflower crudités for dips don't hit the spot – at least they don't for me. Somewhere in between in cooking terms is a glorious vegetable that so rarely has a chance to shine except as the support for a mountain of hot liquid cheese in the classic dish cauliflower cheese. We should all eat more cauliflower cheese and I have given you a broccoli version of it earlier on but these recipes give cauliflower a chance to show its own character.

Cauliflower and green beans

According to 'Jane Grigson's Vegetable Book' the humble cauliflower was first noted in the Middle Ages as an exotic Arabic plant. This book is a mass of vegetable information and good recipes, and it was from here that the cauliflower, green bean recipe came to my attention some time ago. I like it hot but Jane Grigson proposes that it is best served as a cold salad. Either way it is quite nice and highly nutritious.

Serves 2 as a main dish or 4 as a side dish.

1 medium cauliflower
175g (6oz) green beans
Freshly ground black pepper
1 clove garlic
Bunch fresh mint
45ml (3tbsp) virgin olive oil
1 lemon

1. Trim the cauliflower and cook in boiling salted water for no more than 10 minutes. Drain.
2. Top and tail the beans if necessary and cook in boiling salted water in a separate pan for 5 minutes. Drain and arrange with the cauliflower in a shallow dish. Season well with pepper,
3. Scatter over chopped garlic and mint.
4. Mix oil and lemon juice and add the dressing to taste.

This dish can be eaten on its own as a light meal or I like to have the cauliflower and beans with a slice of pizza. How about some grilled or barbecued chicken? Flatten a couple of chicken breasts with your rolling pin, drizzle on some olive oil and grill away. Serve the chicken piping hot with the cauliflower just warm and a glass of red wine (Minervois from the South of France).

Cauliflower fritters

Serves 3 or 4

I haven't much in the way of fried food in the book for obvious reasons, but cauliflower fritters are my exception, so get out the deep fat fryer or the deep frying pan. For once we are living dangerously.

1 large cauliflower
2 egg whites
50g (2oz) plain flour
100g (4oz) breadcrumbs
40g (1½ oz) grated cheese (optional)
Sprinkle of paprika

1. Trim the cauliflower into florets; cook in boiling salted water for 10 minutes.
2. Take 3 bowls, with white of eggs in one, flour in another, and breadcrumbs in the third. (you can use the yolks also but I am trying to keep this healthy – well sort of!).
3. Flour the florets, dip them in egg white and then coat them with breadcrumbs.
4. Deep fry in oil at around 160°C until the outsides of the florets are brown.
5. Remove with a slotted spoon and dry on kitchen paper.
6. Place in a serving dish and sprinkle with cheese and a dusting of paprika on top while still warm. Eat right away.

I have to say these are very much a treat, which we like to eat with a slice of savoury mince pie or cold pork pie with green salad on the side. A white Zinfandel from California would go nicely, especially with the pork pie combination.

Cauliflower pie

This is my type of pie because none of this clever pastry making is needed – just roll out some ready made puff pastry and that's it. Cauliflower pie often came to my rescue at times in my life when money was sparse. It is nutritious, filling, cheap and a fine meal whenever it is eaten.

Serves 2 hungry people – or a meal for 2 with leftovers

1 large cauliflower
1 onion
50g (2oz) butter
35g (1½ oz) plain flour
350ml (11 fl oz) milk
5ml (1tsp) of French mustard
15ml (1tbsp) mustard seeds
2.5ml (½ tsp) ground mace
50g (2oz) grated cheese
30ml (2tbsp) chopped fresh chives
60ml (4tbsp) natural yogurt
350g (12oz) packet of puff pastry
Salt and pepper

1. Chop the cauliflower and use stalks as well as florets (cheap and filling remember); cook in boiling salted water for 3 minutes, then drain.
2. Chop the onion and fry in the melted butter for 1 minute or so and then stir in the flour and cook this for a further minute.
3. Add the milk, mustard, seeds, mace, cheese and chives; stir and let the mixture thicken.
4. Add all the cauliflower, the yogurt and mix.
5. Put the cauliflower and sauce into a pie dish.
6. Roll out the pastry, place over the pie dish, cut to shape and pinch the edges. Make a hole in the centre for steam. Cook at gas mark 6/200°C for 25 minutes. (The pie crust can be glazed with egg to colour).

A few boiled potatoes and some frozen garden peas is all the cauliflower pie needs to make it into a very substantial meal. The filling is intended to be cauliflower in a creamy sharp mix and not cauliflower cheese with a crust so be careful with the cheese – it really just serves to balance the mustard. If the pie has too strong a mustard flavour for you then drop the mustard seeds.

The dish goes quite well with a soft red wine – Dolcetto, an everyday wine from Piedmont in Italy would be my first choice.

Celery

Celery

I am quite weird about celery on the one hand I think it is a great treat to have a few sticks of fresh celery; a little salt and some good farmhouse cheese as a supper, but on the other I have to confess that I just hate celery soup. Don't let me put any of you off liking celery soup – it is nutritious, healthy and definitely good eye food. It's just one of my pet hates and it even makes me queasy just to mention that dreaded soup here. Surprisingly large numbers of people tell me they do not like the taste of celery in any form or fashion; however, it is only the soup with which I have problems.

I was in the West of Ireland staying with my in laws one time and my wife Dee and her parents decided that a pub lunch was in order and we would have soup and bread. I was already feeling like the outsider as of course you are when Mum, Dad and Daughter get together after not seeing each other for a while. On top of that they were talking some kind of 'English' I could not follow and now they were organising me right down to soup and bread! It was time to get petty. 'I'm not sure I want pub soup thank you! I might not like it.' Dee countered 'Oh Ian you like most soups don't be silly.' When faced with the truth all I could say was, 'well I hate celery soup!'. Dee countered immediately, 'Celery soup is very English, I've never had that over here in my life.' At which point my mother and father-in law arrived at our table with piping hot bowls of celery soup.

Celery and cheeseboard

Grapes are an excellent accompaniment to a cheeseboard, but don't forget celery sticks, since they go just as well. I chop the celery into manageable pieces, i.e. 3 pieces per stick, and place them, in a jug or glass at the centre of the cheeseboard, alongside the biscuits. Don't be tempted to cut the celery into matchsticks – that is too much work and detracts from the celery.

1 or 2 heads celery
1 small box savoury biscuits
175g (6oz) French Brie
175g (6oz) Red Leicester
175g (6oz) White Lancashire

1.Wash celery and chop off any leaves if present. Retain the leaves.

2. Cut each stick into two or three pieces depending on the size of head, and place into a jug beside the biscuits and cheese on the cheeseboard.
3. Place no more than three or four different cheeses on the board.

I think cheeseboards can get too fussy. It is much better to have three or four decent sized cheeses than a whole host of little bits. I have gone for a soft cheese, a waxy cheese and a crumbly cheese for variety but that is entirely up to you. They all go with celery and bring the best out of the vegetable. Don't throw away the leaves. They are decorative, good to eat and very healthy. They can go into a vegetable soup or stock if you do not wish to eat them with the cheese. A small glass of late bottled vintage (LBV) port would be enjoyable with this dish.

Waldorf salad

The Waldorf salad started life in the Waldorf Astoria in New York at the end of the 19th century and over its 100 years of life it has undergone many mutations and variations. The basic combination is celery, apples and mayonnaise; well at least two out of the three are good for you! I add some walnuts and a few grapes so we get up to four out of five.

Serves 2 as a salad or 4-6 as a side dish

5 sticks celery
2 green eating apples, such as Granny Smiths
Juice of 1 lemon
100g (4oz) seedless green grapes
10 walnuts
30ml (2tbsp) low calorie mayonnaise
75ml (5tbsp) fromage frais

1. Chop up the celery, getting rid of any stringy bits and place in a bowl.
2. Core and slice up the apples leaving the skin; add to the bowl.
3. Add the lemon juice, grapes and broken up walnuts.
4. Mix the fromage frais and mayonnaise into a dressing; coat the contents of the bowl with the dressing and place in the fridge for 1 hour before serving.

You will find many other mixtures and combinations in recipe books but remember not to get too fancy and stick with a combination of celery and an apple that you like.

A light white wine like German Hock is about right with this salad.

Celery in yogurt

I hope the idea of celery in yogurt does not put you off, although I do admit it does sound like something that would accompany your nut burger after a hard day at the health farm. Quite the opposite, it is good solid food, so give it a try.

Serves 4–6

900gm (2lbs) celery
1 large onion
30ml (2tblsps) virgin olive oil
450ml (3/4 pt) chicken stock
200ml (7 fl oz) plain yogurt
Pepper
25g (1oz) butter
15g (1tbsp plain flour)

1. Cut the celery into short lengths and place in boiling salted water for 5 minutes.
2. Chop the onion and lightly fry in the olive oil for 3–5 minutes in a large pan.
3. Add the celery and chicken stock.
4. Season, cover and cook for up to 30 minutes.
5. Remove celery and place in a serving dish in a low oven, reserving the liquid.
6. Melt the butter in another pan, stir in flour and cook for 1 minute, stirring to stop any sticking.
7. Stir in the stock and the yogurt and bring to the boil; keep stirring until it turns into a creamy sauce. Pour over the celery and serve.

Eat with sliced tomato, a little boiled or fried rice and a thick slice of bread to mop up the juices.

Reds don't usually taste that well with celery or yogurt for that matter, but a straightforward white such as Bordeaux Blanc is good.

Courgettes & Marrow

Courgettes and Marrow

Courgettes are related to marrows and both are a good source of vitamin C and minerals. Courgette is the French name for baby marrow but it is Italy and Italian dishes where courgettes really come into their own. The Italian word for these small marrows is zucchini. Zucchini is the preferred term in the USA and these vegetables have a surprisingly prominent place in American cooking. The marrow is much more the English vegetable that is still grown in many allotments and gardens, usually as large as possible. I think among English gardeners the marrow is often talked about but seldom eaten. They were my Dad's Achilles heel: there was not much he could not grow in his garden but he was rarely successful with marrows. One year he was really determined to beat his jinx and took great care with his planting. I was a small boy at the time, full of curiosity, so I kept asking questions and distracting him. To get me out of the way he gave me a few of his precious seeds and ushered me to another part of the garden. I knew I was being fobbed off, so in disgust I threw the seeds into the compost heap and thought no more about it. As usual Dad's marrows never really took off, but out of the compost heap grew two of the largest marrows I have ever seen!

Fried courgettes

Serves 4–6 The dish is simple and delicious.

4 courgettes
45 ml (3tbsp) virgin olive oil
30 ml (2tbsp) chopped fresh mint
30ml (2tbsp) white wine vinegar
Seasoning

1. Chop the courgettes into slices and fry in half the oil for 6 minutes.
2. Mix the remaining oil with vinegar and the mint and heat in a separate pan for 1 minute or so.
3. Pour mixture over the warm courgettes off the heat and leave for at least 90 minutes.
4. Reheat if required but it can be served as a cold dish.

I do like these fried courgettes warm and it will accompany most meat and vegetable dishes. I happen to like it as a partner with shepherd's pie and peas. The courgettes go well with cold meat leftovers such as turkey and particularly lamb. It is also an interesting side dish at barbecues.

On its own, this dish goes well with American red or blush Zinfandel.

Fruity courgettes

Don't worry, the dish is not as bad as it sounds. In fact I have included it here because, without doubt, it is one of my favourite courgette recipes. It is best to use small courgettes if possible and it is a healthy vitamin C rich treat.

350g (12oz) courgettes
½ lemon
½ orange
6 spring onions, chopped
5ml (1tsp) powdered ginger
30ml (2tbsp) white wine vinegar
5ml (1tsp) sugar
45ml (3tbsp) chicken stock
5ml (1tsp) cornflour

1. Cook the courgettes whole in salted boiling water for 4 minutes. Drain and top and tail each courgette.
2. Grate the lemon and orange, extract their juices.
3. Place these, the chopped onion and all the sauce ingredients except the cornflour in a small pan and boil for 3 minutes; then reduce heat to a low simmer.
4. Blend the corn flour with 2 tsp of water and add to the warm sauce, stirring all the time until it thickens (1–2 minutes). Add sauce to the courgettes in a dish.

The courgettes need to be cooked whole so they don't take up water and they go well with roast chicken or as part of a vegetarian meal.

A small glass of Moscatel de Valencia, an inexpensive Spanish sweet wine, I think goes well with the citrus bite of the fruity courgettes.

Baked marrow rings

Marrow is watery and subtle flavoured. My Mother boils the wedges and serves them with butter and lots of pepper. I prefer to slice them, peel the skin and cut out the centres to make rings; these I cover with a little oil and bake. A few years back I went vegetarian for a while and sometimes hated but frequently enjoyed vege and vegan recipes. I do like stuffed marrow and I love almonds, which are a rich source of vitamins A and E. The recipe is adapted from one I first found on the internet (www.veganfamily.co.uk/marrow).

Serves 2–3

1 large marrow
1 large onion
3 slices of bread
100g (4oz) almonds
30ml (2tbsp) virgin olive oil
Bunch of fresh chopped basil leaves (or 10ml (2tsp) dried)

1. Cut the marrow into slices, peel and cut out the centre with the seeds.
2. Chop the onion roughly and combine it with the bread, almonds and basil in a processor. Blitz until finely chopped.
3. Spoon the mixture into the marrow rings on a baking tray and sprinkle each ring with oil.
4. Bake in preheated oven for 30 minutes at gas mark 5/190°C.

Enjoy these with a generous sprinkling of pepper. The stuffing is an interesting mix of flavours that do not lend themselves to an easy wine choice, so I would opt out and go for a mineral water. There are lots of fillings for marrow rings including cheese and mince.

Cucumbers

Cucumber

We all think of cucumber as a standard sandwich filling and part of a simple salad. As a nation we do eat a fair amount of cucumber but it is considered by many to be a dull, burpy salad vegetable that is eaten automatically rather than with any great enthusiasm. To me cucumber has always been special, maybe partly because my father hated it. Surprisingly, he disliked cucumber not because of its taste but its smell. Personally I don't think it has much smell, but Dad could pick up the whiff of a cucumber half an hour after the last sandwich had been demolished. A great treat in my childhood was tiny cucumber sandwiches with my Mum, when Dad was well out the way! The cucumber was always peeled and cut gossamer thin: 'The way the Queen would have it' was my Mum's explanation, but the real reason was that cucumber was rare and rather expensive in the 1950s.

Salmon strips and cucumber straps

This dish is a favourite of mine. I saw the 'Naked Chef' Jamie Oliver on TV making these marvellous cucumber straps and filling huge plates with them. He then piled on the lemon and then I think added fish of all sorts to the plates. Dee and I had a dinner party the next day and needed a quick and easy help-yourself starter – problem solved. It worked out so well that we do straps of cucumber frequently; usually with smoked salmon as a starter and with the addition of cold fresh salmon as a salad. The other ingredients are up to you but I base the mixture around the dressing that goes on a whole poached salmon at a posh buffet. Remember, however, that the salmon in this dish is the garnish and the cucumber the main attraction!

Serves 4 generously

100g (4oz) mixed lettuce leaves
2 large cucumbers
100g (4oz) smoked salmon
175g (6oz) fresh poached salmon
3 radishes
1 lemon
4 tbsp virgin olive oil
5ml (1tsp) capers
5ml (1tsp) dill weed
Pepper and salt

1. Take a large plate or shallow bowl (we use a cake plate) and spread out the lettuce over the bottom of the dish.
2. Remove the ends and chop each cucumber into three, but do not remove the skin; use a potato peeler to cut straps or ribbons of cucumber down the whole length of the cucumber segment. Each strap will have skin, lining one edge or both edges if you have a wide enough peeler. Spread the straps over the lettuce.
3. Cut smoked salmon into small strips and spread among the straps.
4. Flake the fresh salmon and scatter over the dish.
5. Slice the radishes as thin as possible and spread around the salad.
6. Squeeze the lemon over the dish and drizzle over the olive oil.
7. Scatter on the capers, dill weed, and salt and pepper to taste.

Enjoy with quarters of brown bread. This is very much a cucumber lover's dish, but do give it a try. A more subtle variation is to have only a garnish of lettuce, about 3 cucumber straps, placed on top of a small smoked trout fillet. With a squirt of lemon this is very nice.

The wine to suit the salmon is a French Chardonnay Vin de Pays or an affordable Chablis.

Cucumber and cider

This is a quick dish easily prepared and great in the summer. A surprising number of people who are not that enthusiastic about cucumber take to this dish.

2 cucumbers
150ml (1/4 pint) dry cider 15ml
5ml (1tsp) sugar

30ml (2tbsp) fresh parsley
(1tbsp) fresh chopped chives
Pepper and salt

1. Top and tail the cucumbers, peel and cut in two lengthways; remove the seeds and chop the flesh into thin slices. Put the slices in a bowl and add the cider.
2. Introduce the rest of the ingredients and season well. Stir.
3. Place in the fridge for not less than 1 hour.

Serve with cold meats, cold or warm fish (from sardines to fresh salmon) and any pork dish particularly pork chops. I like the cidery cucumber with a nice pork fillet and some boiled and minted new potatoes.

Cucumber stir fry

We use cucumber too much like a garnish or something you slice and put a little in a sandwich. In Chinese cooking, a cucumber is used in the same way as a marrow or a pumpkin; in other words it is treated as a proper vegetable.

2 cucumbers
Salt
3 spring onions
1 clove garlic
15ml (1tbsp) vegetable oil
5ml (1tsp) ground ginger
2.5ml (½tsp) chilli powder
150ml (¼pt) water
15ml (1tbsp) honey
Sesame seeds

1. Peel cucumbers, cut in half then cut lengthways. Cut into strips, salt and leave for 30 minutes.
2. Chop up the spring onions and garlic.
3. Heat the oil in a deep frying pan and add onions, garlic, ginger and chilli powder. Fry for a few seconds.
4. Add the cucumbers and continue to fry.
5. Add the water and honey and keep cooking until most of the water is gone.
6. Add the sesame seeds and serve.

I do not find cooked cucumber at all indigestible and it does make, when cool, an excellent sandwich filling as well as, when hot, an interesting side dish. Cucumber and pork are good stable mates but I think it works well with cold meats of any sort and cold or hot roast beef in particular.

A glass of Italian Pinot Grigio, one of my wife's favourite white wines, makes the ginger/sweet cucumber sandwich rather special.

Leeks

Leeks

Is it me or do people not eat leeks as they often once did? If that is so, then my family are the exception. We eat loads of leeks but usually in the winter, despite them being an all year vegetable these days. They are such a good vegetable and real 'eye' food because they are full of lutein, antioxidants and minerals. I have loads of recipes with leeks in them but as a plumber once said to me, 'Don't mess about with leeks! (or was it leaks?).' I shall keep to recipes that I think are both simple and effective.

Leek and potato soup

I have to do leek and potato soup because we have it all the time at home and at any time of day from breakfast to supper. On a cold winter's morning Dee (who eats a big breakfast) will even make me (a cup of tea and a juice man normally) relish a bowl of this soup. Also it is a cure-all in our house –'not feeling well? Have some leek and potato soup', 'You have a cold coming on, Eat this soup!' or even 'Had a bad day dear? How about some leek and potato soup.' Try it, but beware you might become hooked like us!

Serves 4 (or 2 very hungry people)

2 large leeks, sliced
2 very big potatoes
900ml (1 1/2 pints) chicken stock
30ml (2tbsp) virgin olive oil
Salt and pepper to taste

1. Heat the oil in a large pan and and the sliced leeks. Fry/sweat the leeks gently for a few minutes without burning.
2. Add in the chicken stock, and the chopped/cubed potatoes and bring to the boil. Simmer, covered, for 15-20 minutes.
3. Blend in a liquidiser or food processor but not for too long; the soup is best left nice and lumpy!
4. Serve in a wide rimmed bowl and enjoy with crusty brown bread.

A white Côte du Rhône or Sauvignon Blanc goes quite well with this soup.

Vegetables à la Greque

This dish contains loads of key antioxidant foods including broccoli, celery and parsley, but the main one is the leek. I first had this as a cold cooked vegetable salad with cold meats, but it is also nice warm with rice.

Serves 4

175ml (6 fl oz) white wine
30ml (2tbsp) lemon juice
5ml (1tsp) olive oil
2 sprigs fresh thyme
2 bay leaves
450g (1lb) or more leeks
4 sticks celery
12 florets broccoli or cauliflower
30ml (2tbsp) fresh parsley
Salt and pepper to taste

1. Put the wine, lemon juice, oil, thyme and bay leaves in a heavy based pot and bring to simmer.
2. Chop the leeks into rings, celery into segments and add to the pan with the broccoli or cauliflower.
3. Simmer for at least 5 or 6 minutes or more until cooked.
4. Remove vegetables with a slotted spoon and then briskly boil the liquid down to half, which will take at least 15 minutes.
5. Add chopped parsley to the reduction and pour over the vegetables.
6. Serve warm with rice or pasta.

Alternatively let the dish cool, then place in fridge for at least 1 hour after which eat on its own or with pies or cold meats.

Any dry or medium white wine will be fine.

Curried leeks with mushrooms

I love curries and that goes back to my days as a student in Glasgow. Next to Chinese, the cheapest night out then (as now I suspect) was in the exotic surrounds of the nearest curry house. Unfortunately my very first venture into an Indian restaurant was doomed to failure. The owner mistakenly thought that, by having Glasgow girls as waitresses, the culture shock would not be so great for his customers (this is in the late 1960s and Glasgow was not renowned for its sophistication).

Four of us, our student grants fresh in our pockets, tentatively entered 'The Bombay Duck'. The music was strange and the menu was even stranger (what is all this Buna and Korma business?). We pleaded with the waitress for help but she said, 'I've only been here two days and it's all nonsense to me also! Have a steak and chips like everyone else!' (I have translated the Glaswegian into English to protect the innocent). Anyhow the owner, who was also the chef, got his own back by drowning everyone's steaks with fierce curry sauce. Little did he know that curry sauce and chips would become a way of life in the not so distant future. Leek curry doesn't sound too promising does it? However, it first came to my attention on the menu of an Indian restaurant where it was entitled 'The best curried leak in East London.' Now that does sound painful. However, it is simple to make and tastes much better than it sounds; I hope you agree!

Serves 4

450g (1lb) leeks
30ml (2tbsp) olive oil
2 cloves of garlic
10ml (2tsps) curry powder
5ml (1tsp) grated or powdered ginger
5ml (1tsp) garam masala
225g (8oz) mushrooms
225g (8oz) creamed coconut (half a tin)
or 100g (4oz) of dry grated coconut instead
15ml (2tbsp) lemon juice

1. Wash and chop the leeks; fry them in a large frying pan with the oil, garlic (crushed) and other spices for 5 minutes or until soft.
2. Quarter the mushrooms and cook them on low heat for a minute or so in the leek mixture.
3. Add the creamed coconut or the grated version with a little water, and continue frying for a further minute.
4. Finish by adding lemon juice.

This quick curry can be served on a bed of rice, or I like it just with a few new potatoes.

Pink wines like Mateus Rosé from Portugal and Anjou Rosé from France are fine with this but Dee prefers a glass of milk with curries.

Welsh pie

My friend Mary Kelley and her family live in a smallholding in Wales and, of course, produce all their own vegetables. She gave me this marvellous recipe for Welsh pie that is a real winter warmer. It makes use of the top greens of the leeks that are very rich in antioxidants and nutrients but are often discarded. In her recipe she adds lashings of cream at the end but I have substituted a little cheese as an alternative.

Serves 1 (if you can get away with it, but otherwise enough for 4!)

1 onion
600g (1 1/2 lb) leeks with tops
200g (8oz) green back bacon
25g (1oz) butter
30ml (2tbsp) olive oil
Seasoning
Few sprigs of parsley
1kg (2 1/4 lb) potatoes
150ml (1/4 pt) chicken stock
50g (2oz) cheese

1. Chop the onion and the leeks (including tops).
2. Chop the bacon into strips, and pan-fry all three in a big pan for 7 minutes in the the oil and butter. Strain and reserve the juices.
3. Season the leek mixture well with pepper and add some chopped parsley. Reserve some parsley for later.
4. Peel the potatoes and slice thinly.
5. Butter a gratin dish and layer alternately with leek mix and potatoes ending with potatoes on top.
6. Salt, then press mixture down.
7. Warm the stock and reserved juices and add to the pie until the stock has reached the top layer of potatoes.

8. Bake at gas mark 6/200°C for 50 minutes until the potatoes are tender and liquid absorbed.
9. Grate the cheese and spread on top with the remaining parsley. Return to the oven for 10 minutes.
10. Serve piping hot in bowls as a one-pot meal.

The cheese is optional but I think rather nice, and I have cut the quantity to the bare minimum. If you are OK with cheese then double up to 4oz for a much better topping. A vegetarian option would be to substitute mushrooms for the bacon and vegetable for the chicken stock. Pickled cabbage and beetroot go well on the side as they do with Lancashire hot pot.

A robust red wine works best, such as a tough southern Italian like Montepulciano.

Notes

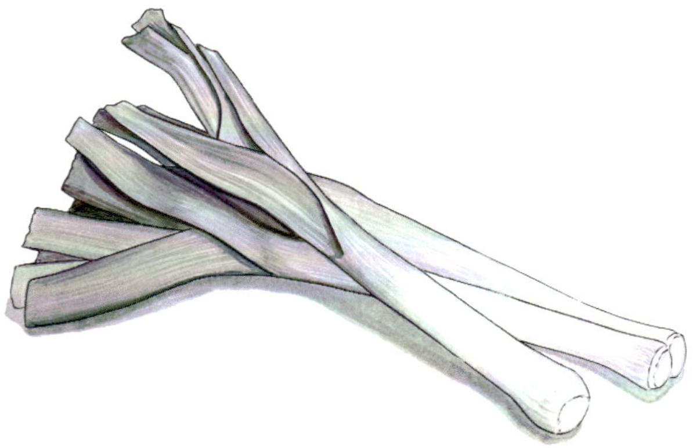

Lettuce

Lettuce

In the past in Britain we have tended not to be very adventurous with lettuce; there was the Iceberg and the other one. Now the supermarket shelves are full of different types; in addition there are packets with all sorts of leaves.

Rocket, pear and cheese

The lettuce need not be rocket but it is nice and peppery so it goes very well with smooth, sweet pears and savoury cheese. The dish is really an alternative ploughman's lunch, but also it is a perfect starter.

Serves 4 as a snack (but it will make a substantial meal for 2)

100g (4oz) washed rocket (or mixed leaves)
3 pears (any type)
1 lemon
15ml (1tbsp) walnut oil or virgin olive oil
35g (1 1/2oz) Edam
10ml (2tsp) sesame seeds

1. Spread the salad leaves in a bowl.
2. Peel and core the pears and then chop them up into the slices.
3. Cover with lemon juice and add the oil.
4. Sprinkle the cheese and the sesame seeds on top and add a good pinch of pepper.

We use any cheese that is around in the fridge and, although I prefer mild cheeses in this combination, Stilton and Danish Blue work well. If you want to add to the dish and make it a special starter, then why not quarter a couple of fresh figs and add them to each plate?

Chicken and mixed lettuce

In the 1980s and 90s a favourite kitchen present was a wok. Stir-frying is fun but not every day and what do you do with the wok when you are finished with it? We never found out and it kept getting in the way. Now our wok languishes in the basement full of grime and rust. I wonder where the Chinese store woks in their small kitchens? The wok did introduce us to a very effective way of quick cooking that seals the goodness into both meat and vegetables. Now we use a high sided, non-stick frying pan that is multipurpose since the wok went into retirement.

Serves 4 for lunch and 6 for supper

50g (2oz) endive
50g (2oz) chicory leaves
50g (2oz) from packet of mixed leaves
350g (12oz) skinned and boned chicken breasts
1 onion
1 clove of garlic
10ml (2tsp) virgin olive oil
1 red pepper, chopped
175g (6oz) mangetout
175g (6oz) can of sweetcorn
15ml (1tbsp) soy sauce
15ml (1tbsp) tomato ketchup
15ml (1tbsp) chilli sauce
30ml (2tbsp) sherry
Freshly ground black pepper

1. Break up the salad leaves and mix together in a serving bowl.
2. Flatten the chicken breasts with a rolling pin, and slice.
3. Crush the garlic and chop the onion.
4. Add the oil to a large frying pan and heat; cook the onion, garlic and meat for 5 minutes moving the contents frequently.
5. Add the pepper, mangetout and corn and fry for 3 more minutes.
6. Mix the soy sauce and ketchup in the sherry and add chilli sauce.
7. Add the sauce to the pan and heat through for 3 minutes coating everything in sauce.
8. Add chicken and vegetable mixture to the salad leaves, mix well.

A rosé wine would be my first choice such as a Southern French Syrah rosé or a Californian Zinfandel blush.

Warm lettuce

Chinese often heat lettuce in the wok as part of their greens. The Chinese lettuce called bok choi is available now in many grocery shops in the big cities that have a sizable Chinese population like London, Manchester and Liverpool. For this dish I use an ordinary Cos lettuce or any lettuce that is firm with a lot of leaf.

Serves between 2–4

700g (1 1/2 lb) cos lettuce
45g (3tbsp) oyster sauce
15g (1tbsp) peanut oil

1. Remove lettuce leaves and add to boiling salted water in a wok or large pan for 30 seconds. Drain when wilted and add to a serving dish.
2. Mix oyster sauce and oil; drizzle over the leaves, serve immediately.

This dish goes with any but the most mildly flavoured meats. Any nut oil will do if peanut is not available.

Braised lettuce

This is an old dish that my grandma would do when there was a glut of lettuce in the garden. Although the lettuce makes a substantial vegetable dish I do think it is an accompaniment to a meal rather than the whole meal in itself. It goes particularly well with lamb chops, roast lamb or any roast for that matter. An ideal companion is grilled lamb's (or pig's) liver. Liver is rich in iron and antioxidants so it is a healthy companion as well as a tasty one.

Serves 4

4 firm lettuce
2 onions
3 large carrots
125g (4oz) streaky bacon
25g (1oz) butter
300ml (1/2 pt) chicken stock

1. Trim the lettuce; blanch in boiling salted water for 2 minutes and drain.
2. Peel and chop the onion and carrots; cut bacon into three slices per rasher.
3. Melt butter in pan and fry the onion, carrots and bacon for 10 minutes.
4. Add lettuce, pour in stock; season and simmer, covered, for 20 minutes.
5. Transfer food to a serving dish and keep hot.
6. Boil the liquid down to a sauce (reduce by half).
7. Pour over lettuce and serve immediately with meats.

To my taste a South African or Australian Shiraz would be nice with the lettuce and liver combination. Remember though that liver is only an option; the dish stands well on its own.

Peppers

Peppers

I shall call the fat colourful peppers, sweet peppers and the ones that burn I will refer to as hot peppers. This section is all about sweet peppers that can be bought in every grocer's shop and supermarket. They are rich in carotenes and therefore are good eye and general health foods. The red peppers have a far higher content of carotenes and lutein than the green ones (as much as 5 times more lutein). They have to be the pepper of choice with respect to eye health.

Roast peppers

Peppers have a completely different texture and flavour when they are roasted. I think roasting works well for all sweet peppers but red peppers are best by far, which is just as well because they are the ones with the most eye-related goodness. The only problem with roasting peppers is getting the charred skin off the pepper. I find the easiest way is to take the piping hot peppers and put them in a suitable plastic bag and close it up. The steam and heat loosen the skin so effectively that it is no problem removing the skin once the peppers have cooled.

Serves 4

3 red peppers
1 yellow pepper
75ml (5tbsp) virgin olive oil
15ml (1tbsp) balsamic vinegar
5ml (1tsp) dried rosemary
1 lemon
30ml (2tbsp) crushed pistachio or other nuts
Seasoning

1. Halve the peppers and clean out the centres.
2. Mix together the oil, vinegar and rosemary.
3. Halve the lemon and squeeze the juice into the oil mixture and stir well.
4. Place the peppers cut surface down in a grill pan without the rack. Brush them well with the lemon and oil mixture,

then grill the peppers until the skins blacken, basting with the mixture frequently.

5. Put the cooked peppers into a sealed plastic container or simply cover them with foil. Let the peppers cool a little then peel the skins off.
6. Put them in a serving bowl and scatter over the nuts and drizzle on any remaining mixture. Season to taste.

Leaving the peppers enclosed to cool helps to loosen the skin further, so that peeling is easier. Roast peppers can be a main dish or a substantial side dish. Why not try the complete roast: roast beef, roast potatoes and roasted peppers (and plenty of gravy)?

Whether you have roast meat with your peppers or have the roast peppers as a main dish with your favourite pasta and some fresh tomato sauce perhaps, go for a decent robust red wine. Roast pepper is one of the few vegetable dishes that is not overwhelmed by a powerful red, so go for a Chilean or Australian Cabernet Sauvignon.

Dee's stuffed red peppers

There are so many different recipes for stuffed peppers but I do think peppers are an ideal edible container. They come in different combinations and vary from the vegetarian onion and mushroom mix, rice or cous cous, through assorted cheesy variations and, for meat eaters, lamb or beef mince, a perfect filling. My wife uses the simplest filling that combines just straightforward breadcrumbs with mixed herbs and black pepper.

Serves 2 as a main meal and 4 as a side dish

4 large red peppers
8 slices of stale bread
7.5ml (1 1/2 tsp) dried mixed herbs
2.5ml (1/2 tsp) black pepper
Olive oil for cooking

1. Cut the tops off the peppers and clean out the pith and seeds.
2. Blitz the bread, herbs and pepper in a food processor until the bread is in small crumbs.

3. Stuff the mixture into the peppers and replace the tops.
4. Put the peppers in a roasting dish and drizzle them with olive oil. Cook at gas mark 4/180°C for 20 minutes.
5. Serve onto a plate when ready.

The stuffed peppers really liven up a bland dinner (mince and potatoes or pork casserole for example) as a side dish, in which case you would only need one each. Have two each if it is a main course with rice or pasta bows. Dee says her recipe is fine as it is, but for a main course I would liven the pepper stuffing up with a couple of salty, chopped anchovy fillets and some grated cheese, but that is entirely up to you.

The easy drinking (and easy on the pocket) red wines of La Mancha in Spain would be my choice to go with the stuffed pepper dish.

Flamenco eggs

Most of us take care how many eggs we eat these days so when we do have an egg then it's got to be a treat. I can't think of a better egg treat than Flamenco eggs – it's an excellent way of making the humble egg that extra bit special. As an added bonus it is easy to prepare.

Serves 2 as an evening treat

2 red peppers
3 tomatoes
½ an onion
4 rashers of back bacon
2 large eggs
15ml (1tbsp) olive oil
Seasoning

1. Chop the bacon into bits.
2. Slice the onion, core and slice the peppers and chop the tomato coarsely.
3. Fry the onion and bacon in the oil for 2 minutes.
4. Add the peppers and tomato and continue cooking for 1 minute.
5. Pour the vegetable mix into an ovenproof dish.

6. Flatten the mixture and make two hollows with the back of a ladle. Crack an egg into each hollow.
7. Place the dish on the middle rack of an oven preheated to gas mark 6/200°C. Cook for 10–15 minutes depending on how well set you like the eggs.
8. Serve immediately with crusty cob rolls.

I like the eggs to have runny yolks so I would not cook this dish beyond 10 minutes but by 15 minutes the yolk is hard and the vegetables are as well done as you would want.

An Italian Barbera would be my choice of red wine but whites made with the Viognier grape (southern Rhône Valley and California) are also good and probably a better match.

Pepper and tomato stew

Sweet peppers mix brilliantly with tomatoes and both are great eye and general health foods. Red peppers are a sound source of lutein and beta carotenes in general. They are rich also in the antioxidants vitamins C and E. Tomatoes have lots of vitamin C and, although they are poor in lutein, they have plenty of betacarotene. The Griersons often holiday in the Costa Blanca which is where I first met this colourful red stew that doesn't take long to cook. The Costa Blanca, like many parts of the Spanish coastline, is full of Brits and there is some interesting mixing of tastes. In one British restaurant I know in Alicante they serve the stew with lovely 'imported' Lincolnshire sausages.

Serves 4 people as a main dish or 6 as a side dish

30ml (2 tbsp) virgin olive oil
1 onion
3 large red peppers
1 small green pepper
4 plum tomatoes
1tsp sugar

1. Heat the oil in a decent sized pan.

2. Slice the onion and cook for 1minute.
3. Core and chop the peppers into strips and cook for 5 minutes.
4. Remove the tomato skins by placing in boiling water and then peeling.
5. Chop the flesh roughly and add to the stew with the sugar. Simmer for 6 minutes or a little longer until tender.

I think the pepper and tomato stew is perfect on its own served in a bowl with thick bread but the sausage idea is sound – ideal with good pork sausages like Cumberland.

I prefer red wine with a dish that is dominated by peppers and would choose a Californian Merlot.

Notes

Spinach

Spinach

Spinach has always been considered to be good for you, almost medicinal. Its extremely high lutein and iron contents support that view. On the down side over the years it has had few fans in the favourite food department. Like many medicines it can look and taste awful. Certainly, if you buy spinach as that green gook in tins (that Popeye eats), it does not look so nice nor is it as nutritious as fresh leaves. With a little care and the right recipes it can be a great vegetable, especially if it is not overcooked. Gently cooking the leaves in stock (sweating) imparts extra flavour, and spinach goes extremely well with two spices in particular: ground nutmeg and ground cumin.

Salad Niçoise with spinach

A long time ago before I came to Merseyside, I quite liked the idea of working in Canada. Picture the scene: I was being interviewed outside a waterfront restaurant in Vancouver looking out over the Pacific Ocean. My host, who would have been my boss, asked me what I would like to eat – 'the same as you please' was my sucking-up-to-the-boss kind of reply. It turned out to be a simple salad niçoise, but the green stuff was baby spinach leaves rather than iceberg lettuce. No, I didn't take the job in the end, but I still remember the delicious salad enjoyed in the warm Canadian sunshine and, yes, people often think I am mad!

Serves 2 generously and can be stretched to serve 4

450g (1lb) waxy potatoes
225g (8oz) French beans
900g (2lb) fresh spinach leaves
1 large tomato
1 hardboiled egg (optional)
100g (4oz) olives
5ml (1tsp) capers
1 garlic clove
60ml (4tbsp) virgin olive oil
15ml (1tbsp) balsamic vinegar
5ml (1tsp) lemon juice
15ml (1tbsp) fresh chopped parsley
6 anchovy fillets

1. Peel and chop the potatoes and cook in boiling water until just tender.
2. Top and tail the French beans and cut into short lengths.

Cook those until tender (or better still buy a tin and chop and cook them the easy way!).

3. Make a nest of washed spinach leaves (pat dry with paper towel) in a large bowl. Spread in the chopped potatoes, tomato, egg, beans, olives and capers.
4. To make the dressing, mix the crushed clove of garlic, olive oil, balsamic vinegar, lemon juice and parsley in a small bowl. Add pepper to taste. Mix well and pour onto the salad.
5. Place the anchovies on the salad; leave out the egg if you have a cholesterol problem.

Enjoy with crusty bread and a nice bottle of white wine – Canadian Riesling or a Muscadet from France might be nice.

Garlic spinach

The trouble with my job is that I have to go all over the world – what a drag! I'm joking of course. One time in Singapore, I went out into the old China Town late at night, when it was cooler. I had been talking about eyes and eye problems all day and had forgotten to eat. I was starving and the cooking smells in China Town were unbelievable, as was the noise! There were sizzling woks and the hum of many conversations every where you turned. I've eaten garlic spinach many times but this night in Singapore it never tasted better! Eat it at home with pork or lamb chops and some nice boiled potatoes.

Serves 4 as a side dish

900g (2lb) fresh spinach leaves
30ml (2tbsp) peanut (or olive) oil
2 garlic cloves
5ml (1tsp) lemon grass oil (fresh ginger will do instead)
15ml (1tbsp) dark soy sauce
10ml (2tsp) brown sugar
Pinch of salt (optional) or nutmeg (optional)

1. Cut out the thicker stems from the spinach leaves. Wash and dry with kitchen towels.

2. Heat the oil in a wok or large frying pan (peanut has a better flavour than olive oil for this).
3. Add chopped garlic and lemon grass oil and stir for a few moments then add the spinach. It is one of life's miracles that a huge amount of leaf can sweat down to very little in 2 or 3 minutes!
4. After 3 minutes add the soy sauce, brown sugar and salt.
5. After 3 or 4 minutes the spinach will have taken up all the flavours and is ready for the plate.

It you are having lamb chops and potatoes with the spinach then prepare them first and keep them hot in the oven while you stir-fry the spinach.

Red wines go with the chops, perhaps Cabernet Sauvignon best of all, but white wines match with the spinach such as an Italian white like the ever popular Frascati.

Spicy marrow and spinach

We are off to another exotic part of the world for this recipe: how about Old Street in North East London? I used to work in Moorfields Eye Hospital on City Road and near by is Old Street. Old Street has some of the old East End nostalgia, pubs and markets and the like, mixed in with overspill offices from the financial end of the City. It is an unlikely place for a long-standing vegetarian restaurant, which is now a health food shop. I will always remember the restaurant for spicy marrow and spinach served piping hot by girls in Doc Martin boots, jeans and spiky hair.

Serves 2

450g (1lb) (around half) a marrow
30ml (2tbsp) olive oil
10ml (2tsps) cumin seeds
5ml (1tsp) or a pinch of chilli powder, depending on taste
30ml (2tbsp) water
450g (1lb) young fresh spinach leaves
90ml (6tbsp) singlecream
Salt and lots of freshly ground black pepper

1. Cut marrow flesh into cubes.
2. Heat the oil in a large frying pan and add the cumin seeds and chilli powder (to taste).

3. Add marrow cubes and the water to the hot pan, cover and cook for at least 2 minutes or until most of the water is gone.
4. Wash the spinach and tear into rough bits removing any thickish stalks. Add to the marrow and cook gently for 1 minute.
5. Stir in the cream; cook on a higher heat for a further 2 minutes.
6. Add lots of pepper and a little salt and it is ready to eat.

Vegetarians would have this as a main dish with rice. We carnivores might grill up a gammon steak and have that as well.

For the Veggies the wine has to be a white wine from Alsace like Pinot Gris, but German Liebfraumilch is a lot cheaper and just as good. For the carnivores amongst us an Australian Grenache might be better.

Fish florentine

This is not an Italian dish, I believe it is French and basically it is fish or eggs on a bed of spinach. Florence was at one time renowned for its high quality spinach so I guess the name of the dish pays homage to that historical superiority.

Lunch 2–3 for lunch

450ml (3/4 pint) fish or vegetable stock
30ml (2tbsp) white wine
675g (1 1/2 lb) young spinach
50gm (2oz) butter
2 lemons
6 skinned plaice fillets
Pinch of ground ginger
Seasoning

1. Heat half the stock with a little wine in a large pan. Add all the spinach and let it wilt down and cook (5–8 minutes).
2. Remove and layer the spinach in a buttered gratin dish. Sprinkle with half the juice from one of the lemons and keep in the oven on low heat.
3. Meanwhile season the plaice with salt, pepper and ginger.
4. Roll the fish up and secure with cocktail sticks. Simmer in stock and the juice of the remaining half lemon for 10 minutes.
5. Arrange the rolls of cooked fish on top of the spinach and use the remaining lemon for garnish.

Quarters of thin buttered toast are a welcome addition, as is a dry white wine like a South African Colombard.

Spinach and chick pea mix

The spinach and chick pea dish involves one-pot cooking and I think it originates somewhere in North Africa. Certainly that is where I first tasted it. The mix combines diverse flavours and textures, but it is dominated by the spinach and chick pea combination. Sometimes it also contains ladies fingers (okra) that I have left out. It is full of flavour, and in North Africa it is made in a great big pan for communal eating. I have to say that, if you are ever involved in communal eating where everyone dips in with their right hand with lumps of bread, it is best not look too closely at the fingernails! This dish is a favourite of mine despite the memories of all those hands in the communal pot.

Serves 3 very well but can be stretched to 4

1 onion
1 clove garlic
45ml (3tbsp) olive oil
5ml (1tsp) turmeric
5ml (1tsp) cumin powder
5ml (1tsp) curry powder
3 tomatoes
400gm (14oz) (2 tins) of chick peas
200ml (7 fluid oz) chicken stock
50g (2oz) raisins
400g (14oz) baby spinach leaves
Seasoning

1. Peel the onion and garlic and chop. Add to the oil in a large heated pan and cook for 2 minutes.
2. Add the spices and continue cooking for another 3 minutes.
3. Chop the tomatoes and add to the pan. After a couple of stirs add the chick peas and the stock and bring to the boil. Cover and simmer the mixture for 5 minutes.
4. Add the raisins at this point, then add the baby spinach leaves and allow them to wilt for 5 minutes.
5. Season well. Serve as a main course with crusty cob or naan bread.

Leave the curry powder out if you must, but the cumin is essential as it gives the basic flavour to the stew. I like to drink a nice cheap white wine with this dish – southern Italian or Sicilian white is good.

Sweetcorn

Sweetcorn

Obviously corn is not a green leafy vegetable but it does have in common with the GLVs a high lutein content so it is a 'must have' vegetable for those of you who want a high dietary intake of carotenes. It is eaten far more often in the USA than in the UK, where, in many States, it is a staple food. I think that we don't really know what to do with it except to use a tin of corn as a rare alternative to tinned peas or beans. I don't think the British really are all that comfortable with corn on the cob especially when it is leaking rivers of molten butter. Grabbing the cob in two hands and slobbering over red hot kernels of corn is just not in our nature! I have an abiding memory of my Mum and her friends, dressed in their best clothes, trying to be delicate with corn on the cob on a plate, and absolutely refusing to pick them up!

Although corn is a healthy vegetable, I have to say that most of my corn recipes are a bit too rich in butter, eggs and cream. Even the ones I have selected are rather too rich in calories and cholesterol to be any more than occasional treats.

Corn on the cob

Corn on the cob seems to demand lashings of butter, but I have had it with a sweet and sour sauce that is almost as nice and it is definitely a little healthier.

Serves 2

50g (2oz) dried apricots
1 red pepper
1 small onion
2 celery sticks

150ml (1/4 pint) malt vinegar
30ml (2tbsp) tomato ketchup
60ml (4tbsp) demerara sugar
15ml (1tbsp) corn flour

1. Chop the apricots, pepper, onion and celery and place in a small pan containing water. Bring to the boil and simmer for 30 minutes. Strain and reserve the liquid.
2. Make a paste with some of the liquid and the cornflour.
3. Put the vinegar, ketchup and sugar in a pan with the cornflour

paste and bring to the boil. Keep stirring until this thickens to a sauce.

4. Cook the corn on the cob in boiling water for 20 minutes, adding some salt at the end of cooking time.
5. Serve 2 cobs per person with sweet and sour sauce on the side.

A white wine on the sweet side such as German Riesling Spatlesse goes well with the sweet and sour.

Sweetcorn fritters

Sweetcorn fritters are an American delicacy that they have alongside fried chicken. The classic chicken and sweetcorn dish is Chicken Maryland. Normally the fritters would be cooked in a deep fat fryer but I have a fear of those things. Instead I use my deep frying pan but still shallow fry.

450g (1lb) large can of sweetcorn
1 large egg
50g (2oz) plain flour
½ lemon
15ml (1tbsp) olive oil
45ml (3tbsp) vegetable oil for frying
10ml (2tsp) powdered parmesan cheese
Seasoning

1. Drain the corn.
2. Separate the white from the yolk of the egg.
3. Put the flour, grated lemon rind, pinch of salt, olive oil and egg yolk into a bowl. Stir into a smooth batter.
4. In another bowl, whisk the egg white until stiff.
5. Fold the corn, egg white and batter together.
6. Heat the vegetable oil in deep frying pan (or fryer) and when hot add spoonfuls of corn mixture. Turn once during frying – about 5 minutes.
7. When finished season with some powdered parmesan and pepper. Eat immediately.

The fritters are made to be eaten with roast or fried chicken. They also go very well with turkey, pork fillet and a host of other meats. How about trying roast chicken on a bed of mixed lettuce, a baked potato with low fat coleslaw and corn fritters?

A nice glass of Californian Pinot Noir would set the meal off nicely.

Sweetcorn and crab soup

This is a classic Chinese soup that I think tastes wonderful and reminds me of the best part of exotic Chinese banquettes. Having said that I think this soup is special, I have to admit that I have never made it with 'real' sweetcorn and crab meat. In my house it has always been concocted from the contents of two tins!

Serves 2 for lunch

1 egg
5ml (1tsp) sesame oil
1litre (1¾ pts) chicken stock
15ml (1tbsp) soy sauce
5ml (1tsp) ground ginger
5ml (1tsp) sugar
Seasoning
280g (10oz) tin of sweetcorn
10ml (2tsps) cornflour
225g (8oz) tin of crabmeat
6 spring onions

1. Crack the egg, separate the white from the yolk and set the yolk aside. Make up a mixture of the egg white and sesame oil.
2. Boil up the stock in a large pan.
3. Add the soy sauce, ginger, sugar, seasoning, sweetcorn and simmer.
4. Blend the cornflour in 10ml of water, add to the soup and cook for 5 minutes.
5. Add the crabmeat.
6. Pour in slowly the oil/egg white mix while stirring the soup.
7. Chop the spring onions and garnish the soup. Serve in small bowls.

A white wine with a bit of acidity is needed for sweetcorn soups and I would go for Australian Verdelho. On a totally different tack you could put the alcohol in the soup rather than a glass. Add a little dry sherry to give the soup an extra lift but only a little sherry is needed.

Tomatoes

Tomatoes

At the end of summer in the town of Buñol near Valencia in Spain the townspeople hold their Tomatina festival. The object of the festival is for the young and not so young to hurl in excess of 100 tons of tomatoes at each other. 'No bad thing' some might say 'tomatoes don't taste like they used to'. True, unfortunately, due to intensive farming, but they are still extremely nutritious, as they are a good provider of vitamin C and the key source of the carotene called lycopene (see Table 3).

The intense smell, flavour and colour of the tomatoes of days gone by had a lot to do with the great care taken over them by farmers and gardeners alike. My Uncle Jim was a very enthusiastic tomato grower. The secret of his very tasty tomatoes was the contents of a water butt outside his greenhouse that he called 'liquid gold'. We kids thought that gold had to be unlimited pocket money. So one afternoon three of us wrestled with the lid of the butt. Unfortunately we prized it free and were drenched with muck. Liquid gold consisted of all sorts of things but the main constituents were blood, liquid manure and bone meal. Uncle Jim was furious that we had wasted so much of his secret formula but that was the least of our worries. We were sure we were going to die from some gruesome disease and we smelled so bad that we were half convinced the imagined disease might be a merciful release!

Tomato and mushroom salad

A friend of ours from Columbia does an excellent but simple tomato and mushroom salad. I think plum tomatoes have a really nice flavour and make an ideal salad along with cherry tomatoes that have a nice sweet taste.

Serves 4 for a starter or lunch

6 plum tomatoes
10 button mushrooms
24 cherry tomatoes
45ml (3tbsp) virgin olive oil
10ml (2tsps) white wine vinegar
Salt and freshly ground black pepper

1. Chop up the plum tomatoes and slice the mushrooms.
2. Cut the cherry tomatoes in half.

3. Spread slices of tomato and mushroom over a flat dish.
4. Mix the vinaigrette (roughly four parts oil to one part vinegar) and sprinkle some over the salad.
5. Season and serve immediately.

This salad is ideal fresh and should be eaten immediately after making it as a starter or as a side dish. It can be a side dish to almost anything, but it does accompany light meats rather well such as cold chicken and potato croquettes, or even your standard fish and chips.

A dry white wine such as Sauvignon Blanc or a Semillon Sauvignon Blanc mix would be my first choice but any white would be fine. If you prefer red then it would need to be very light.

Tomato pie

This is a real tomato hit and I think it is easier to make two pies at once. You can use fresh tomatoes but I never have done so for this dish. Good tinned chopped tomatoes make this recipe easy but don't use the cheap tins. Treat yourself to the ones with good flavour: you get what you pay for. I don't make the pie cases either but buy them from the supermarket ready made.

50gm (2oz) grated cheese
2 short crust pastry cases – size 20cm (8ins) (or make your own)
30ml (2tbsp) olive or vegetable oil
2 onions
2 cloves of garlic
2 x 400gm (14oz) tins of chopped tomatoes
50g (2oz) tomato purée
Salt and pepper to taste
1x 280g (9oz) jar of white asparagus spears
125g (4oz) of black olives halved (optional)

1. Place the grated cheese in the pastry cases and warm in a low oven gas mark 1/140°C.
2. Heat the oil in deep pan and fry the chopped onions and garlic for 2 minutes.

3. Add the tomatoes and purée; simmer for about 25 minutes.
4. Season the thickened mixture and add to the pastry cases.
5. Arrange the asparagus on the tomato in rows or a lattice pattern.
6. Increase oven temperature to gas mark 4/180°C and cook for 10 minutes.
7. Remove pies and spread the halved olives on top as an optional garnish.

I like a slice of this pie hot with a baked potato; however, it is fine eaten cold with a green salad. Black olives are not everyone's favourite and they can be omitted, or why not sprinkle on a few fresh basil leaves or button mushrooms instead?

A nice Australian oaked Chardonnay would go down well with the pie.

Fish and tomato sauce

Our little boy ate reasonably well at table for a 2-year-old (which meant food was not flying in all directions at all times). On the other hand he rated a family meal out at a restaurant on the same level as a visit to church on Sunday – something to be endured with as many treats and as much noise as possible. His main treats in a restaurant were tomato sauce (ketchup) and chips, at the sight of which he would start shouting 'sawss, sawss sawss' and even more embarrassing 'fork'n knife, fork'n knife' which was his cry for cutlery. If anyone met us in a restaurant I would have to say lamely, 'My little boy is not swearing honestly!' Of course he wouldn't go for a real tomato sauce and was not convinced it even was tomato sauce, no matter how hard I tried to convince him otherwise.

Serves 4

150ml (¼ pint) of fish or vegetable stock
5g (1tsp) black peppercorns
Bay leaf
½ lemon
4 cod, or any fish steaks
400g (14oz) tin of chopped tomatoes
1 clove of garlic
12 stoned black olives
5ml (1tsp) capers
Seasoning

1. Heat the stock in a large pan and add the crushed peppercorns, the bay leaf and a squeeze of lemon.
2. Add the fish steaks to the liquid and simmer for 10 minutes; remove and keep warm. Cover with lid or tin foil.
3. Pour the tomatoes into a medium pan; add the chopped garlic, black olives and capers; season well.
4. Cook for 15 minutes adding in the stock for the last 5 minutes. Raise the heat to reduce the sauce if required.
5. Serve some of the sauce into each of the four bowls; add a cooked fish steak to each and serve.

I know cod is getting more and more expensive; on the other hand any white fish steak will go with the tomato sauce. A little white wine can be added to the tomato sauce on special occasions and a white wine that I like with a rich tomato flavour is the classic grape from the Alsace region of France with the funny name of Gewurtztraminer.

Pizza salad

It is not only the youngest boy who has a thing about tomatoes. My eldest boys are now in their 20s but, when they were teenagers, their favourite meal by far was pizza. Pizza restaurants were the only place to go for a meal out. At home, 'What would you like to eat for dinner?' was a rhetorical question. The restaurant in the hospital where I work has a pizza which is a burnt offering on a concrete base, but even that was not safe from the 'pizza mob' when they visited me. Frequently I tried to wean them off the pizza and one of my attempts was a mozzarella, tomato and leaves salad. It didn't work for them at the time and they named it the 'pizza salad with grass'. None the less it is an excellent salad that is full of goodness and antioxidants, so I hope you try it out. It is also dead simple and quick to make.

Serves 4 as a starter

200g (7oz) from a packet of mixed salad leaves,
200g (7oz) cherry tomatoes
125g (4oz) mozzarella
15ml (1tbsp) virgin olive oil
5ml (1tsp) balsamic vinegar
Freshly ground black pepper

1. Spread the leaves over a salad bowl.
2. Halve the tomatoes and scatter in the salad.
3. Remove the mozzarella from the liquid and slice thinly before mixing in with the rest.
4. Mix the oil and vinegar and drizzle over the salad.
5. A couple of turns of the pepper mill and the salad is finished.

I now know this to be a classic Italian salad but at the time I thought I had come up with something clever – how thick can you be? With this healthy salad, a Verdicchio is pleasant but any dry white Italian wine will do.

Notes

Turnips, Parsnips & Swedes

Turnip, Parsnips and Swedes

Turnips are little white peppery vegetables whereas swedes are large with orange flesh. Shouldn't be difficult but the Scots, and as you know by now I am one, traditionally call swedes turnips, and Swedes are people from a country in Scandinavia. To add to the problem, swedes are also called neeps in old Scots. My parents lived in Scotland but my mother is a Londoner, so total confusion reigned in our house. On Burns Night 'bashed swedes' rather than 'chapped neeps' were the gruesome accompaniment to haggis (or was it the other way round?).

I do think all three of these root vegetables are desperately underrated by the general public. Again school dinners and bad pub lunches have done nothing to further their cause. It has to be said that our tendency to eat all three when they are too big and have gone coarse has not helped. Equally the need by many of us to mellow their taste with lashings of butter and cream has given them black marks with nutritionalists and health experts.

Swede and parsnip mash

Swede is associated with the Burns Night festival in Scotland but in my youth I remember them most at Halloween when they were not for eating! We used to get the largest turnips (sorry swedes) we could find and hollow them out to make lanterns in the same way the American children use pumpkins. Lantern competitions were common but my abiding memory was the terrible smell produced by the hundreds of candles burning the insides of all these neeps!

Enough for 4 people

1 medium to large swede
4 big parsnips
45ml (3tbsp) semi-skimmed milk
25g (1oz) butter or margarine
Seasoning

1. Peel the swede and cube.
2. Scrape the parsnips and slice leaving out woody parts.
3. Add both to a large pan of salted boiling water; simmer for 20–30 minutes.

4. Drain well and mash with a potato masher adding milk and knobs of butter until smooth.
5. Add pepper and salt to taste and serve.

We have this mash with Sunday lunch and it is a great favourite. The swede and parsnips can take up a lot of butter and milk and look and taste better and better, so if calories and cholesterol are important to you be careful!

Turnip rings and parsnip twigs

As you will have gathered long before now my cooking is not rocket science and this is dead simple stuff but I think it is very effective. The trick is to make the slices thin but not too thin. The slices get placed on a baking tray and shoved in the oven in the same way as the roast potatoes.

3 young (spring) turnips
4 parsnips
Virgin olive oil
Pinch of dried parsley and/or mixed herbs
3 sprigs of thyme

1. Scrub and peel the vegetables. Slice turnips into rings that are about 1cm or more and the parsnip into batons 6–8cm long and ½–1cm thick.
2. Coat the baking tray with oil; sprinkle oil and herbs onto the vegetables.
3. Place in the oven at gas mark 6/200°C for 20 minutes; turn half way through.

Dee loves to do these with the Sunday roast and often places them in with the roast potatoes. If you make them too thin they will form crisps but the crisps go very well with chicken, duck and even game birds.

Turnip and vegetable pie

This pie is by no means exclusively a turnip pie, and it is topped by potato rather than pastry. Essentially it is a mixture of earthy vegetables and root vegetables, but turnip is a key taste. All the rest can change depending on what you have available but nice peppery white turnips need to be there. I mix and match all the time with this dish so I have listed the mix I used last – just a week ago!

Serves 4

4 medium to small turnips
175g (6oz) broccoli
1 onion
2 large carrots
75g (3oz) green beans
50g (2oz) butter
25g (1oz) plain flour
300ml (1/2 pt) chicken stock
150ml (1/4 pt) semi-skimmed milk
5ml (1tsp) dried parsley
175g (6oz) mushrooms
1 red pepper
8 medium potatoes
60ml (4tbsp) natural yogurt
50g (2oz) cheese
5ml (1tsp) of sesame seeds
Seasoning

1. Peel and cube the turnip; break up the broccoli into florets, peel and slice the onion and carrots; top and tail the green beans and cut themin half. Cook all these in salted boiling water for 10 minutes; drain and rest.
2. Melt the butter in a pan and stir in the flour vigorously; cook for 1 minute. Remove from the heat and add the stock and milk. Boil the liquid until it thickens.
3. Add the cooked vegetables, the dried parsley plus the chopped mushrooms and pepper.
4. Peel and cut up the potatoes; boil for 15 minutes in salted water. Drain and mash with a little butter and the yogurt adding in most of the grated cheese and the sesame seeds.
5. Pour the vegetables and sauce into a dish and cover with the potato mix. Scatter the remaining cheese and seeds over the top.
6. Cook for 30 minutes in the oven at gas mark 5/190°C.

I like to have this dish as a meal in its own right and it is certainly sufficiently substantial for that. As we have a mixture of carnivores and vegetarians in our family, this is a useful dish. The vegetarians have a large portion whereas the carnivores have their meat and the pie as a side dish. Grilled, or baked with the pie, pork sausages go very well, as does a brown beef stew or even a chicken casserole.

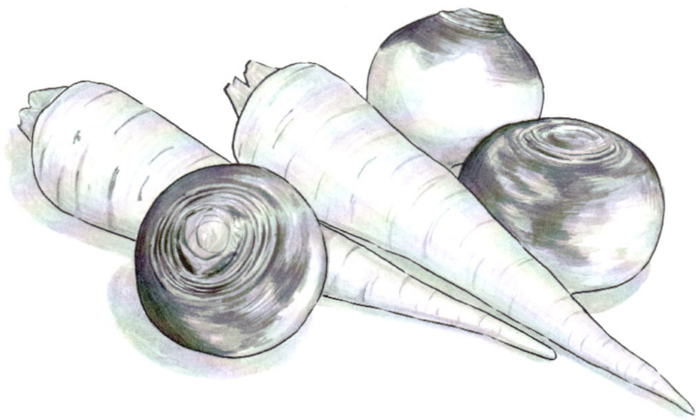

I like the aromatic white wines of France's Rhone Valley such as Viognier if I have the pie as a main meal.

Watercress

Watercress

Watercress is packed with iron and vitamins and it has a high lutein content to boot! A 100g helping will give you twice the vitamin C you need per day and about 70% of the necessary vitamin A. The problem is that it is eaten mostly in little bits and pieces more as a garnish than as a vegetable in its own right. I want to make a case for eating lots of it and not just leaving the greenery on the side of the plate after a good meal.

Watercress salad

Watercress goes brilliantly with walnuts and the combination of the two together with a nice dressing makes a pleasant side salad.

Serves 4 generously

½ a Cos lettuce
1 stick celery
85g (3oz) watercress
5ml (1tsp) peppercorns
5ml (1tsp) mustard seeds
1 clove garlic
45ml (3tbsp) virgin olive oil
15ml (1tbsp) balsamic vinegar
Pinch of brown sugar
Pinch of salt
200g (7oz) walnuts

1. Break up the Cos lettuce and spread the leaves in a salad bowl.
2. Chop up the celery and add with the watercress to the bowl.
3. Crush the garlic, pepper and mustard in a pestle; add the oil, vinegar and sugar to make the dressing and sprinkle over the salad.
4. Sprinkle on the salt and crushed walnuts and serve.

Try out some of the salad mixture in a sandwich of white or whole meal bread. A very cold glass of Asti Spumanti will make the sandwich complete, particularly on a lovely summer's day.

Watercress sauce

I have kept away from vegetable sauces in this book because often the goodness of the vegetable is offset by loads of butter and cream. I didn't want to delude you into thinking that, because they contain a healthy vegetable or two, creamy sauces are good. The usual advice is either to use calorie-rich sauces sparingly or substitute oil and milk for the butter and cream. This home-made watercress sauce is far better than the shop variety, even when I have substituted milk for cream.

Serves 4 generously

2 spring onions
1 stick celery
30ml (2tbsp) olive oil
120ml (8tbsp) white wine
75ml (5tbsp) vegetable stock
1 bay leaf
150ml (1/4 pint) milk
170g (6oz) watercress

1. Chop the spring onions and celery finely; fry in the oil for 2–3 minutes.
2. Add the wine, stock and bay leaf to the pan; simmer for 2 minutes.
3. Add the milk and chopped watercress and bring up to heat for 2 minutes.
4. Blitz until smooth in a liquidizer. Reheat and serve.

The sauce goes very well with grilled fish of any kind and also it works well with roast chicken.

Salmon and watercress

Dee and I often abuse this dish. It is often top of the list when we have a visitor and it is necessary to whip something together as soon as possible. I say abuse because salmon and watercress are actually an excellent and healthy combination that are a classic in their own right and deserve far more respect than we usually give them. Alongside the many beneficial attributes of watercress, fresh salmon is equally impressive in terms of health benefit. Salmon is a good source of omega 3 fatty acids that protect against heart disease and an equally good source of vitamin A and carotinoids for the eye.

Serves 2 as a main course

225g (1/2 lb) small new potatoes
2 salmon fillets
5gm (1tsp) peppercorn
4 spring onions
Pinch of salt
1 lemon
85g (3oz) packet of watercress
100g (4oz) crème fraîche

1. Scrub the potatoes and put them on to boil in salted water until tender.
2. Parcel up the salmon fillets in tin foil and add whole peppercorns, chopped spring onions, some sea salt, a couple of drops of water and lemon juice. Crimp the parcel closed and cook in an ovenproof dish for 15 minutes at gas mark 4/180°C.
3. Spread the watercress over the plates; then lay a cooked fillet, with the onion and juices on each plate.
4. A good dollop of crème fraîche will finish the plate off.

I think this is a lovely meal. It is clean, colourful and full of goodness. What more could you want except perhaps a nice cold glass of white or rosé wine. My first choice has to be a nice very dry Chablis.

Watercress pâté

I love pâté from a rough farmhouse to mackerel but most of them are so full of unsaturated fats that they should carry a government health warning. The problem is that it is the butter and fat that makes a pâté so special. For that very reason vegetable pâtés, unless soused in pork fat or clarified butter, just don't quite get there. Watercress pâté nearly makes it but not quite. Do try it however, and even though it makes me yearn for the real thing, it is still very good on squares of hot toast. It is also very easy to make.

1 onion
1 clove garlic
15ml (1tbsp) olive oil
300g tin chopped mushrooms
200g packet of watercress
120g of cottage cheese
15ml (1tbsp) soy sauce
½ lemon

1. Chop the onion and garlic. Heat the oil in a frying pan and fry the two until the onion is clear.
2. Add the mushrooms, then add the watercress and allow it to wilt down. The whole frying time is less than 5 minutes.
3. Put the contents of the pan into a blender along with the cottage cheese and soy sauce. Blitz until the mixture is smooth.
4. Put the pâté in the fridge for 2 hours or until needed.
5. Serve with lemon wedges and toast.

A glass of Australian Riesling would be my choice if I was having this pâté as a starter at a dinner party.

Fruits

Fruits

I have spent my time in this book extolling the virtues of vegetables with hardly a mention of fruit (I know that tomatoes are considered a fruit but to me they are a vegetable!). This has been deliberate because fruit sell themselves to the public whereas vegetables, and GLVs in particular, get ignored in the shops or, when they are served up in a meal, they get pushed to the side of the plate. Vegetables are in dire need of a public relations effort, whereas fruit does not need PR to the same extent. It is not the case that vegetables are better for general and visual health than fruit. Fruits are stars in their own right and we should all eat fresh fruit every day – it is not one or other, it is both together.

So it goes as read that fruit is good for you and essential to a healthy diet rich in the antioxidant vitamins, carotenes and minerals that are required for the retina and the macula. For example, cantaloupe melons, which are in most supermarkets and high street greengrocers, have lutein levels way beyond most vegetables and all but the best of the GLVs.

Sugar fruit

No I am not even going to try to pretend that sugaring fruit is in any way good for you but I think they are very yummy and an ideal (well almost) pudding substitute for those of you with a sweet tooth who need a sugar fix at the end of a meal. I'm a black forest gateaux and banoffie pie man myself so I need some sort of half way house. If you want complete aversion therapy then my wife and her best friend are recommended. They once made steamed pudding for a poor unfortunate visitor where they used salt instead of sugar in the pudding mix. If this were not bad enough they made up a packet of savoury sauce instead of white sauce for the accompaniment. The visitor and my wife's friend are now an item so it can't have tasted as bad as it sounds, or perhaps love is without taste buds as well as being blind? Needless to say I like to make dessert in our house.

Serves 4

8 satsuma segments
8 canned pineapple chunks (dry them off)
8 strawberries
8 seedless grapes
350g (12oz) granulated sugar
8tbsp water
Cocktail sticks

1. Prepare the fruit segments – peel the satsumas and drain the pineapple chunks.
2. Place all the sugar and water in a pan, and dissolve the sugar over a low heat, stirring constantly. Then boil until syrup browns a little.
3. Take off the heat and then pick the fruit pieces up and dip into the syrup.
4. Let the fruit set on non-stick paper and keep in a dry, cool place.

You can use any segments of fruit you like but I do think it works particularly well with satsumas and strawberries. I prefer pineapple chunks to the real thing because it is so much easier, and a whole pineapple would give you too much fruit. It is nice to serve the fruit chunks in bonbon cases but that is not necessary.

Melon and strawberry

No matter when you eat this light meal, it tastes like summer time. It combines the goodness of cantaloupe melon, strawberries and green salad vegetables. The dish takes me back to a time when I had been working in an Egyptian hospital in the height of a different kind of summer, with little in the way of air conditioning. I felt like I was being roasted alive. Even at night there was little respite except to go off to a local sports and social club. My one and only sport was to find a table in the restaurant immediately beneath a fan and order slices of ice cold melon, surrounded by mixed fruits and drowned with frosted lime juice. Such behaviour can be lethal to the sensitive European stomach – soft fruits are often washed in the polluted water of the river Nile. I have no excuse except to say that at the time I was too hot to care. The present dish is adapted from that Egyptian treat, which I thought of as a life saver!

Serves 2 for a light lunch

1/2 lettuce
1 cantaloupe melon
1/4 cucumber
225g (8oz) strawberries
125g (4oz) green grapes
2 limes
5ml (1tsp) sugar
Mint leaves

1. Spread the chopped lettuce leaves over the base of a serving bowl.
2. Cut up the melon and cube the flesh.
3. Slice the cucumber into sticks.
4. Chop the strawberries and grapes in half.
5. Add all to the bowl and squeeze in the juice of the two limes.
6. Sprinkle the sugar and torn mint leaves over the dish.
7. Cool in the fridge until ready to serve.

The dish is neither a pudding nor a salad but a bit of both and I think works best as a light lunch for two.

A glass or two of the Italian wine Lambrusco will help keep the conversation flowing and both of you nice and cool on a hot summer's day.

Spanish salad

I do not know the correct name for this salad but I associate it with Spain and that is as good a name as any. It combines oranges and baby spinach leaves. We know the value of spinach for eye health, and among USA nutrition experts, the orange has been voted the top fruit and it's high up the list of the top 10 healthiest foods. Olives and pine nuts are rich in vitamin E. Equally important is that this combination tastes fresh and good.

Serves 4 as a starter or supper dish

packet of baby spinach leaves
4 oranges
1 onion
24 olives
packet of pine nuts
5tbsp olive oil
2tbsp wine vinegar

1. Spread out washed spinach leaves in a serving bowl.
2. Peel the oranges, divide into segments and mix them in.
3. Chop onion roughly and add with the olives to salad.

4. Roast pine nuts on a tray under the grill. When cool add to salad.
5. Mix the vinaigrette and spoon over the salad bowl.

This needs to be eaten right away. Satsumas can be used instead of oranges. The professionals would slice out the orange flesh with a sharp knife but I just peel. The salad works whether the oranges are sweet or sharp.

A nice dry sherry goes well with the Spanish salad.

Quick fruit mix

Fresh fruit salad can take a long time to prepare if you let it and it can get really fiddly. We try to take as much sting out of the process as possible by preparing the fresh fruit as easily as possible. The odd can of tinned fruit added in also makes for an easier life!

Serves 6

1 lemon
1 banana
1 eating apple
1 ripe pear
2 kiwi fruit
2 oranges
440g tin of lychees
10 dried apricots
225g (1/2 lb) green grapes

1. Squeeze the lemon juice into a bowl. Add the fruit as you prepare them to prevent discolouration.
2. Chop up the banana; core the apple and chop into segments.
3. Cut the pear into thin circles.
4. Peel the kiwi fruit and slice into circles.
5. Peel the oranges and segment.
6. Open the tin of lychees and mix the fruit and juice with the rest of the fruit in the bowl.
7. Chop the apricots into 3 or 4 pieces and add to the rest.
8. Finally, add the grapes and put in the fridge until needed.

The fruit mix is fine for two or three days. Instead of lychees you can use any tinned fruit. If it is too sweet then add more lemon or even lime juice. Eat with ice cream or sorbet of choice. An Australian Orange Muscat is a favourite dessert wine of mine.

Dried fruit casserole

Dried fruits are extremely nutritious as the water, but little of the goodness, has been lost. Often the only dried fruit many of us ever eat is the content of a mince pie at Christmas or the occasional currant bun. If you fall into that category then you are definitely missing out. When I was a lad, dried fruit meant only one thing and that was the dreaded prune. Prunes and custard were the order of the day if constipation was suspected in any member of the family. My grandma seemed to have particularly virulent batches of dried prunes that were only brought out on these special occasions.

Now there is a wide range of dried fruits readily available and you don't have to enter the inner sanctum of a health food shop to get them these days. They have a special flavour, and this pudding dish uses a mixture of different fruits. Give the dish a try – it is definite comfort food without the after effects of grandma's special prunes. Buy the ready to eat varieties otherwise they require soaking before use.

Serves 6 (or 3 helpings for 2 of you)

125g (5oz) dried figs
75g (3oz) dried peaches
50g (2oz) dried prunes
50g (2oz) dried apple rings
25g (1oz) sultanas
600ml (1pint) of orange juice
5ml (1tsp) ground cinnamon
5ml (1tsp) ground ginger

1. Mix the dried fruit together in a casserole dish.
2. Pour over the orange juice and mix in the spices.
3. Bake in oven at gas mark 4/180°C for 30 minutes.
4. Set aside and allow to cool. Serve in small dessert bowls.

The fruit can be served hot or cold but I think it is much better cold with a little vanilla ice cream. I can't bring myself to have it with custard. Too many old memories!

Here is a chance to have a nice cream sherry or perhaps you might like a small glass of Old Oloroso, the real Jerez product.

Concluding Remarks

In this book I have tried to convince you of three things. The first is that eating more vegetables is a sensible move because there are dietary components that are particularly important for effective vision. The second is that preparation and cooking of vegetable dishes need not be either a lengthy or a complicated process. The third is that even dyed in the wool meat eaters can find vegetable dishes that taste yummy to them. I have to say that, if you select a vegetable dish as a main course in a restaurant, in my experience the lack of meat is usually compensated for by lashings of butter and cream. It is not just restaurant owners and professional chefs that assume that the only good vegetables are those buried in calories. Most TV cooking programmes and, for that matter, all but the most diet conscious recipe books manage to slip a lot more cholesterol into their vegetables than is really healthy.

Without any shadow of a doubt, cream, butter, eggs and fatty meats do combine miraculously well with the textures and flavours of certain green vegetables. A great favourite of mine, but rarely eaten by me these days unfortunately, is an omelette filled with spinach and cream! Avocados are so rich in good oils that eating them on a regular basis is reputed to reduce blood cholesterol. However, all the advantage can be lost if the avocado is drowned in high calorie cream cheese. Fatty bacon bits transform brussels sprouts or cabbage, and melted butter in profusion is a classic companion for fresh asparagus. An Irish doctor and cook whom I know well once said about asparagus that it was such a saint of a vegetable it could be surrounded by sinners. Well it sounds good but it is not at all sensible if taken to extreme!

Like many glib statements there is a grain of truth in it. Simply taking in vitamins and essential minerals does not mean that they are absorbed by the body. In fact a criticism of oral supplements is that the uptake efficiency of some preparations has been proven to be extremely low. However, absorption can be improved if vitamin supplements are taken with appropriate foods. For that matter it is believed by a number of nutritional biologists that far better incorporation of fat-soluble vitamins like vitamin A and E from vegetables is achieved if there is a little additional fat as part of the meal.

The last thing I wish to do is propose that you eat more vegetables for healthier eyes but ignore calorie and cholesterol excess. Think of it more in terms of paying tribute to the old adage that a little of everything in moderation is best and it is usually common sense to avoid extremes. My choice of recipes ignores those that are excessively rich but my selections retain a little fat particularly where I think it brings the best, in terms of flavour, out of the vegetables.

I could be criticised by some of you for my wine recommendations. However, as I have said elsewhere in this book, it is not my intention to turn any of you, and most particularly any AMD sufferers, into alcoholics. A little wine such as the phenol-rich red wines can do some good. Unfortunately vegetable-dominated meals tend to go best with white and rosé wines rather than the healthier 'rough' reds. As a result my recommendations have been predominately whites that make the best 'match', but where a red is possible I have gone for one.

I hope you have enjoyed at least some of the recipes and if you have any comments I would be delighted to hear from you either by letter or email.

Professor Ian Grierson
Unit of Ophthalmology,
University Clinical Departments,
Duncan Building, Daullby Street
Liverpool L69 3GA

Email: ian.grierson@ntlworld.com

www.eyecharity.com

Note: Cauliflower and green beans (page 63) by permission. Jane Grigson's Vegetable Book. Publishers: Penguin 1970.

Index

If you would like more information about macular degeneration please contact:

MDS Helpline: 0845 241 2041

website: www.maculardisease.org

The Macular Disease Society
PO Box 1870, Andover, Hampshire SP10 9AD